Vintage Feasting

Also by Joy Sterling

A Cultivated Life

Vintage Feasting

Joy Sterling

POCKET BOOKS
New York   London   Toronto   Sydney   Tokyo   Singapore

The quote by Eleanor McCrea originally appeared in *University of California/Sotheby Book of California Wine* by Doris Muscatine, et alia, copyright 1984 The Regents of the University of California. It appears by permission of the University of California Press.

POCKET BOOKS, a division of Simon & Schuster Inc. 1230 Avenue of the Americas, New York, NY 10020

Sterling, Joy.
  Vintage feasting / Joy Sterling.
     p. cm.
  ISBN: 0-671-52776-2
    1. Iron Horse Vineyards.   2. Wine and winemaking—California.
  I. Title.
  TP557.S734   1996
  641.2'2'09794—dc20   96-21052
                                                          CIP

First Pocket Books hardcover printing October 1996

10 9 8 7 6 5 4 3 2 1

Interior Design: A. Rosenblatt

Printed in the U.S.A.

To my family

Acknowledgments

I have begged, borrowed, and stolen from the best: Forrest, my parents, Laurence and Terry, Dan Green, Emily Bestler, Rob Akins, Gerald Asher, Marty Bannister, Maralee Beck, Howard Bulka, Craig Camp, Jeff Dawson, Judy and Gary Fishman, Alan Gordon, Robert Glazer, Larry Immerman, Tim Kirwan, George Marrone, Mark Miller, Sidney Moore, Anne Opotowsky, Stephen Pyles, Martin Sinkoff, Larry Stone, Robert Squier, and Josh Wesson.

Vintage Feasting

Introduction

This is a book about how a vintner enjoys wine and what we find so compelling about it. My first book, *A Cultivated Life*, was about growing wine and centered on the vineyards and the winery. This one is about drinking wine and focuses on the table. Where the first describes a year in the life of a vintner as winegrower, this is about the life of a vintner as wine lover—drinking, eating, and living.

Vintage Feasting is about the way my family enjoys wine when we're with company, family, friends or just home alone when my husband, Forrest, and I love to sit on the floor, eat dinner with our fingers, and use dishtowels for napkins.

Vintners are people who love to drink wine. It's why we are involved in this all-absorbing and, we believe, life-enhancing work. Winegrowing is essentially farming, with the same inherent risks and unpredictability.

That's why they say it takes a madman to grow the vine, a wise one to tend it, a lucid poet to make wine, and a lover to drink it.

All of our meals naturally complement wine, which is not an ornament or status symbol but an organic part of our lives. How we choose a wine is usually based on what we're going to eat, though sometimes we pick the wines first and design a menu to complement them. Sometimes the best food and wine combinations are experiments with unexpected results.

Wine can easily turn a simple meal into a spontaneous feast, like a backyard grilled steak with a great Cabernet. The occasion doesn't have to be fancy or stuffy. Our idea of a summer feast is a huge platter of sliced tomatoes—all different kinds—and scattered fresh basil, drizzled with our own extra virgin olive oil, crusty French bread that we can pull apart with our hands, and a delicious Sauvignon Blanc to wash it down. Basically we feel wine is an affordable luxury, one of life's permissible pleasures, and even the highest-quality wine can be enjoyed in the most relaxed settings.

We consider every day a feast day. For a full year, we compiled our most memorable menus and recipes as we created and devoured them. The ones we ultimately chose to include in this book are from real occasions enjoyed at Iron Horse when everything—the food, the wine, and the people—just clicked.

I have recommended many different wines, not just ours—from everyday selections to drop-dead elegant ones.

The menus I've chosen fall naturally in the calendar year, and the wines progress just as they would at a dinner party, from sparkling wines in January to dessert wines in December.

This, I warn you, is a multivintage book. Most of my stories come from 1994 with some 1993 and 1995 blended in. More than 75 percent are 1994, so by strict federal labeling laws I could call it straight 1994, but the other years fill out the book, making it richer and rounder. One of the important lessons of 1994 for me was that you can't look at any vintage on its own.

I initially chose 1994 because it seemed like a typical year at Iron Horse, with the normal ups and downs. At the start of my writing, it was too early to tell what the year would be like, viticulturally or personally. All I knew was that my sister-in-law, Terry, was pregnant, my mother was scheduled for a knee replacement operation, and we were looking forward to celebrating my father's sixty-fifth birthday in October.

The book is divided into months. Each one naturally revolves around meals—just as our life does, surrounded by the season's flowers and fruits and vegetables in the gardens. The menus highlight wine's congeniality with food and are tied to a different theme about wine each month—the smell of wine, the language of wine, the basic characteristics of each wine variety, why wines made from the same grape taste so different, and how you can pair wine and food to please your own tastes—all of which I hope will dispel many of the common inhibitions about wine and show what it is that we as vintners find so wonderful.

The food at Iron Horse is fresh, local, and seasonally abundant. My father has devoted over ten acres of our property to vegetables, fruit, and herbs. Living in Sonoma County, we have the luxury of buying directly from farmers. Many Sonoma products—like fresh oysters, Sonoma baby lamb, and local cheeses—are becoming available nationally. However, we have tried in devising our menus to be sympathetic to the home cook who doesn't have all day to find the more exotic ingredients—lime thyme, a farm-fresh egg, or, for that matter, the extravagance of a vine-ripened tomato, which we have at our fingertips four months of the year.

Many of the menus and recipes are written by our chef Mark Malicki. Mark has been at Iron Horse for five years. He hails from New Haven, Connecticut (famous for its pizzas), apprenticed at Le Périgord in New York and the River Café in Brooklyn, studied with French cooking teacher Madeleine Kamman, attended the Thai cooking school at the Hotel Oriental in Bangkok, and owned his own nationally acclaimed "wine country" restaurant, Truffles, in Sebastopol, before joining our winery. He makes his own cheeses and cures his own meats. Few of Mark's recipes are spontaneous. This year he made prosciutto, which he says is easy— all you need are ten months and a place like my father's wine cellar to hang the hams.

As a counterpoint, there's Forrest's cooking. Forrest

cooks much as he makes wine, instinctively and passionately, without recipes.

I don't know the first thing about cooking. Before Forrest, the kitchen was the coolest place in my house. I used to hide my jewelry in the oven because no one would think of looking there and it was inconceivable it would ever be turned on. I am, however, a world-class eater. The joke in my family is that I eat like a bird—a pterodactyl.

My favorite trophy from my first book is a dust jacket that a friend from Boston sent back to me covered with wine stains. I hope people will read this one the same way.

Lay of the Land

Iron Horse is a marriage of two vineyards—my family's property in Green Valley and Forrest's T-bar-T ranch in Alexander Valley. My parents and Forrest founded the winery in 1978. The grapes from the two estates come into the one winery and are bottled under the Iron Horse label.

The weather is coolest to the west, due to coastal fog, and becomes warmer as you head north and inland. It's about 20 miles to Forrest's property and about 10 degrees warmer than it is at home. The two vineyards are as different as night and day. Even the grapes are not interchangeable. We grow Chardonnay and Pinot Noir at the home vineyard and Sauvignon Blanc, Viognier, Cabernet Sauvignon, Cabernet Franc, Merlot, and Sangiovese at T-bar-T. We couldn't get Cabernet to ripen properly at Iron Horse because of our cool climate, and Pinot Noir would probably explode from the heat at T-bar-T. This climate variation is what allows us to make such a broad range of wines.

We now have 250 acres in vine. We are completely estate bottled, which means we use our own grapes exclusively, producing about 40,000 cases of wine a year. We used to tease Forrest that we could only be as big as however many acres he could walk. Now he has to run.

No two years are alike in the vineyards. Standing behind the winery, looking at the lay of the land, you can see why one side of a hill will yield a completely different taste than the other because of its exposure to the sun, the way the water sheds, or the way the fog settles. Blocks A, B, and C at the foot of the property are often our favorites for still Chardonnay because they lie on a west-facing incline and receive the last rays of sunlight at the end of the day. Different soil types run in bands or ribbons all around the property. What surprises me is how the same section of vineyard will taste different from one year to the next—not just in a good vintage versus a bad one but in two equally fine years. They're just different in the same way that a bed of flowers doesn't replicate itself petal for petal each time it blooms.

How a Vintner Enjoys Wine

My parents became vintners because they love wine, primarily with food, which is the way most people experience it. Their first bottle of wine together was Lancers on their second date in 1951. My father felt very sophisticated ordering wine with dinner. My mother says the best part was that she could take the bottle back to her dorm and put a candle in it.

I don't remember my first taste of wine. The story is that I cut my teeth on brandy. My Grandpa Joe, a dentist, advised my mother to rub Cognac on my gums when I was teething. His only specification was that it had to be the best Cognac.

Justine and Barrie, my nieces, had Iron Horse even before mother's milk. It was the first thing to touch their lips in the delivery room. We view this as progress in my family.

We drink wine with lunch and dinner. We usually

drink our own wine, though not exclusively. My father has a beautiful if somewhat diminished cellar from our years in France. Forrest and I like to reciprocate when my parents come to our house by serving whatever the wine writers and the retailers are touting as the hot wine of the moment. We always serve Iron Horse for guests, though.

Our greatest pleasure is bringing unlabeled bottles to the table. It reinforces the concept of wine as an agricultural product and as an everyday household beverage. It also heightens the feeling that our guests can drink heartily because there's plenty more where the first bottles came from.

If we need a wine for a specific course, we can always create it. My dad wanted an Iron Horse wine for dessert or to accompany foie gras—presto, Demi-Sec, a sparkling wine with a sweeter dosage. Dosage is the finishing element of sparkling wine and at it's most basic sets the degree of sweetness to dryness by how much is added.

Matching food and wine is like painting. Most of the formulas follow basic color theory. Complementary colors, flavors, and smells, musical notes for that matter, all blend naturally. Opposites are vibrant and exciting. Every artist develops his or her own palette—color combinations that reflect the artist's sensibilities. Van Gogh, for example, talked about painting sunflowers with the gusto of a Marseillais eating bouillabaisse.

Forrest thinks of wine as a spice, or more precisely, a multitude of spices. Part of what makes wine so special is that it delivers a broad spectrum of flavors. Different wines with the same dish will create completely separate experiences. In the south of France, sitting by the window at Tétou, a fish restaurant on the beach in Golfe Juan, gazing at the Mediterranean, we indulge in bouillabaisse and quaff ice cold Domaines Ott rosé like it was water. In California, we serve a rich, golden Chardonnay with bouillabaisse. These two wines are not as opposite as they seem. A sturdy rosé is close in weight to a full-bodied white and there can easily be three or four appropriate wines for the same dish, including some lighter reds.

The reverse is also true. Different dishes with the same wine will make the wine taste different. It's like standing in front of a Jackson Pollock wearing a red jacket. All the reds pop out. Change to blue and the whole painting seems to shift. It's an alchemical reaction. Think about how lamb and rosemary combine, merge into one, and then join with yet another element, Cabernet Sauvignon, for example, to create a third, wholly new flavor.

Foods and wines can be matched aromatically, which is one reason why Gewürztraminer, with its perfumed apricot and ginger nose, is often recommended with Asian cuisine.

You can also think in terms of textures—the weight of the food and the weight of the wine—to either counterbalance or complement one another. Friends of ours in Paris always served spinach soufflé and an ethereal rosé champagne for Sunday lunch in the spring. In win-

ter they served a full-bodied red Burgundy with cassou-
let. A classic example of matching food and wine on
weight is Beaujolais with steak tartare versus Cabernet
with grilled steak.

The way the table is set completes the picture. How
food looks on the plate and how wine shines in the
glass definitely make both taste better. The combination
of Brut Rosé and Easter ham is beautifully color coordi-
nated. It's part of the entertainment, as is a well-planned
menu. The right combinations can stimulate or soothe,
express the self, pay homage to a friend, be sexy, impressive, nostalgic, thematic, even artistic. Pairing foods
with a variety of different wines can be one of the most
creative aspects of a meal.

Mark, our chef, once prepared a dinner to honor
Frank Geary, who was then designing the new Disney
Concert Hall in Los Angeles. The menu was an homage
to Geary's work. Mark cut out paper representations
of the food he wanted to serve so he could build the
presentations to look like Geary sculptures. He called
the salad "collision salad" and had the busboys tossing
radicchio, sliced beets, and carrots across the kitchen
to give it a perfectly "deconstructed" look. The main
course, poached salmon, looked so much like one of
Geary's pieces—he is famous for enormous, outdoor
fish sculptures—that it was a little scary. The "scales"
on the fish were thinly sliced potatoes, and the fish
was supported on a pedestal of matchstick potatoes. It
reminded me of a Japanese banquet where every plate
is supposed to hold special meaning, and the food itself

is molded into detailed scenes, with vegetables carved to look like sailboats on a lake near a bridge, all intended to evoke certain memories. Overly manipulated food can often be tasteless, but at the Geary dinner the fish was delicious. We served it with our Pinot Noir.

The rules about matching wine and food used to be very strict: white wine with fish; red wine with meat. But those rules no longer apply, primarily because we don't cook or eat the same way anymore. The classic French menu is a thing of the past. Now, whether it's dressed down or formal, food, like fashion, is multicultural, a mix of French, Italian, Mediterranean, Californian, Asian, and Southwestern. Not so long ago, everything was very structured, just as there used to be fashion dictates. Today people are asking what wine to have with Chinese food. What wine goes well with salsa. It's not just chicken and Chardonnay, but which style of Chardonnay, depending on how the chicken is prepared. The combinations and permutations are endless. And anything goes.

Still, there are certain basics, standards that endure, like champagne or Sancerre with oysters, red Burgundy with roast beef, Beaujolais with steak tartare. Another gambit is to match the wines and foods of an area— Chardonnay, or the French equivalent, white Burgundy, goes well with chicken and Dijon mustard, and it's not surprising that Sangiovese, the Tuscan grape, is delicious with tomatoes. It stands to reason that the wines and foods of a place would evolve together, but that doesn't mean you shouldn't enjoy white wine with beef stew, if that's what you like.

In the face of so much freedom, the one guideline I can think of for planning a menu, including the wines, is that the sequence should build so that you never yearn for the previous course. Its progress should have an inner logic and a rhythm. When the French maître d' says *"Très bien,"* his compliment indicates that you've ordered well so that each course relates to the next and each wine is chosen as a prelude to the wine that follows. In Greek harborside cafés, the waiters applaud if you order in the right progression from fried minnows, which you eat like popcorn, then red mullet the size of a man's thumb, then bigger and ever bigger fish, following the food chain. A natural wine crescendo would be sparkling to Sauvignon Blanc, followed by Chardonnay, Pinot Noir, then on to Cabernet Sauvignon and lastly sweet wines. We tend to drink white to red, dry to sweet, younger to older, though, of course, there are myriad exceptions. Foie gras with Sauturnes is a classic combination; Alsatians enjoy white wine with lamb, and the Bordelais encourage red wine with oysters as they make so little white and Bordeaux extends to the water at Arcachon. I have even enjoyed Zinfandel with oysters—lightly steamed and served with an onion puree and a Zinfandel cream sauce.

Forrest says the key is self-reliance, finding what you like and believing in your choices. And the only way is to taste and experiment. It's like playing the piano; the more you practice the more freedom you'll feel. The good news is that nothing you pick will be truly horrible. Wine writer Gerald Asher says that in all his years he has never tasted anything that ruined a good glass of wine, and with today's technology, the caliber of even the most common wines is far superior to what the kings of France ever dreamed of drinking. Pasturization alone was a major advance in preserving wine.

One secret to avoiding disaster is to taste the wine you are going to serve while you're cooking. You can tailor a dish or alter a sauce to fit the wine perfectly. For example, our chef cuts down the amount of salt he uses when cooking to showcase our wines because their acidity seems to enhance the flavor in food, whereas Jerry Comfort, the chef at Berringer Winery in Napa, says he uses more salt in his dishes.

And even if we assume the worst, that you have undermined a young Merlot by serving it with sugar snap peas, so what? Just push the sugar snaps aside, take a bite of bread or sip of water, and finish the wine.

Everyone tastes differently. It has to do with mouth chemistry, how many taste buds you were endowed with at birth, what you had for breakfast, your mood, and the circumstances. For me, nothing could mar the pleasure of sitting in a café as a teenager living in Paris in the 1960s, enjoying a glass of wine and a pâté sandwich (when I was supposed to be in school), even though the wine was Algerian plonk brought in by tanker. Baron Philippe de Rothschild in his autobiography said that as the owner of Château Mouton he was often asked to name his favorite wine, but his stock answer was that he couldn't pick just one. He said, if the time and place were right and the woman beautiful, then certainly that wine would be the best ever. Conversely, when we see a couple arguing in a restaurant my mother hopes to God they're not drinking Iron Horse because they'll never enjoy our wines again.

Wine is a subjective product. Knowing what you like is all that matters. Certain wines go in and out of fashion. Old-vine Zinfandel is quite the rage right now, while Chardonnay is suffering some reverse snobbism from experts weary of Chardonnay's dominance as the world's white wine of choice. I am in no position to judge whether a magnum of 1870 Château Lafite-Rothschild is worth $17,500. And yet I believe that quality is perfectly objective. There are reasons why one wine costs x and another y. According to Gene Moore, Tiffany's window designer for thirty-five years, "true connoisseurship is being able to recognize quality even if it's not to your taste."

Two things I like to know about a wine are where the grapes come from and who are the people behind it. Therein lies the romance. The best wines have the most delicious stories.

In tasting, I look for finesse, balance, length, and distinction. Finesse is a mark of craftsmanship. It refers to the smoothness of the wine, which is primarily a function of how lightly the grapes were pressed immediately after harvesting. The more lightly pressed the more delicate the juice. Obviously, also the lower the yield and therefore the more costly. Finesse is one reason why one wine is worth more than another.

Balance in a wine means you cannot pick out or separate any of the components—grape blend, alcohol, oakiness—just as you don't see a painting as 20 percent red and 40 percent blue. You want the various elements to blend into one statement, one harmonious expression, and, as we know from art and architecture, balance can be achieved in many ways.

Most experts agree that length—how a wine finishes— is an important aspect of quality. The longer the flavor of a wine lingers in your mouth the better. A short finish is disappointing, like a yacht that's sleek in the front but chopped off in the back because the owners ran out of money.

Distinction in a wine comes from the vineyard, what the French call *goût de terroir,* literally taste of the land, which is an all-inclusive term referring not just to the soil type but to everything about the land—the topography, climate, and exposure. The techniques of premium winemaking are universal. To say today that our Chardonnay is barrel fermented is like saying our milk comes in cartons. The only thing that's proprietary to us are our grapes. To me, a wine that displays vineyard distinctiveness and vintage variation is part of why I'm willing to pay more for it.

For Forrest, the texture of a wine is the difference between good and great. He thinks that a very good wine has a great nose, is full of really wonderful fruit, and has a fabulous finish. It's crisp and juicy, but you wish that the middle were richer. A great wine has a completeness in the mid-palate, a fullness that is totally mouth filling but not unctuous. In an Alsatian wine, the taste should just drench your mouth. Sparkling should be so creamy it practically effervesces away before you can swallow it. Cabernet-based wines at their best are velvety—rich, smooth, and supple.

Every wine has a distinct temperament. My theory is that each one has a particular personality that suits the drinker. It's a twist on the expression "You are what you eat." One of the axioms from the eighteenth-century gastronome Brillat-Savarin is: "Tell me what you eat and I will tell you who you are." I'm sure the same applies to what you drink. It is something like being able to tell the difference between a Rolling Stones person and a Beatles fan.

Champagne or sparkling wine is a drink for optimists. It suggests a positive frame of mind and spontaneity. It's made for immediate consumption, like fireworks— to be shot off all at once. It's a vote for romance and sophistication. James Bond establishes his identity in *Casino Royale* by ordering an older vintage of Taittinger Blanc de Blancs with caviar, tournedos, and *fraises de bois*.

Pinot Noir is for thinkers. It is subtle, challenging, elusive—you have to look into the wine to discover its many nuances. Forrest says Pinot Noir is winemaking's equivalent of Sisyphean struggle: In some vintages you get the wine just right, and in others the rock rolls all the way down to the bottom of the mountain. That's one reason why winemakers call it the heartbreak grape.

There's also a certain earthiness to Pinot Noir. A winemaker who comes to a Pinot tasting without purple hands and mud on his shoes is not taken seriously. In Burgundy, the *vignerons* will test your mettle by taking you through the worst cobwebs in the cellar to the farthest, funkiest barrel. You end up asking yourself, Am I really going to drink out of that?

Merlot, according to Jack Stuart, the winemaker at Silverado Vineyards in Napa, is a wolf in sheep's clothing. Cabernet-based wines are more up front, flamboyant, and aggressive. The shape of the bottle is fittingly broad-shouldered. Zinfandel is a gutsy wine and Zinfandel producers have to be very focused.

Chardonnay's chief virtue is its versatility and adaptability. The Chardonnay vine will give good fruit and reliable wine in many different climates, which has made it synonymous with white wine around the world. In an excellent location, its fruit will mirror the sum total of all the environmental phenomena, what the French call *terroir*. At its best, Chardonnay has the ability to extract unique flavors from each soil and location in which it is grown.

On the other hand, Chardonnay also responds beautifully to all kinds of winemaking techniques, inviting winemakers to design and execute very individual wines. All fine wines are about diversity, but I think this is truer of Chardonnay than any other wine.

Most people do not drink only one wine. My father

prefers different wines with particular dishes depending on the time of the year. Laurence says his choices would also depend on the occasion. Forrest loves all wines. Part of his personality is to be naturally very curious — he always wants to see what's on the other side of the hill, and to try every kind of wine.

What I love most about wine is everything that goes with it, especially people. I am always surprised by the friends we make when we bring the wine. Wine brings people together by providing a common ground. Wine and talk seem to go together as intrinsically as wine and food. The Greek symposiums were originally wine-drinking parties.

Wine is meant to be shared. That's why it comes in the size bottle it does. I can't imagine drinking a great bottle alone. The one story to the contrary that I know is about Richard Nixon, who, according to Woodward and Bernstein, would have a different wine served to guests while his glass was filled from a bottle of Château Margaux wrapped in a napkin to hide the label.

M. F. K. Fisher wrote that food and wine is an art form "which may be one of our last grips on reality, that of eating and drinking with intelligence and grace in evil days." For me, food and wine are simply pleasures, like dancing, smelling a flower, or listening to music, which I hope no one would be denied. Life cannot be all sackcloth and ashes, and looking at the calendar for the new year, I am struck by the number of official reasons to celebrate — recognized, sanctioned feast days — and that's not counting personal occasions like birthdays, anniversaries, the launching of a new wine, and the first flowers of spring, or just because it's Thursday. How sad to be world weary and jaded. To be bored, to tire of caviar, strikes me as truly sinful. Our daily mantra is to remember how lucky we are.

There's a certain etiquette to receiving food and drink. The first rule is to have an appetite. It doesn't matter if you're content just to taste, or are trying to lose weight or are just plain stuffed from traveling and entertaining. When someone offers you a feast you should relish it. Every chef I know looks at the plates when they come back into the kitchen, and if one person doesn't finish everything, they want to know what's wrong.

Last fall we had a very special dinner at The Mansion on Turtle Creek, in Dallas. Chef Dean Fearing was like a mother hen, coming into the dining room with each course to make sure everything was just right. When the entree was served—Texas wild lamb with dried apricot–corn bread stuffing and ancho chili-Syrah sauce, roasted carrots, molasses squash compote, and Iron Horse 1985 Cabernets—Dean stood behind me, picked up my fork and knife, put them in my hands, and said, "Are you talking or eating?"

We vintners feel a little differently. We are quite used to people spitting out our wine at tastings or taking just a sip from a glassful. It's not as much of a waste as it seems. You have to pour a certain amount in a glass to get a complete smell impression and to us it is more important that you taste different wines rather than drain each glass. Here at Iron Horse we encourage our guests to empty their glass on the gravel or in a flowerpot, so they can move on to another wine.

I eat and drink professionally. Some days it feels as though I am pushing away from one table just to move on to the next. I get no sympathy at home. If I complain at all, Laurence will say, "Oh, poor baby. Particularly long lunch today?"

I am partially saved by the French Paradox. The French have long been noted for being able to hardly exercise, eat cheese and foie gras, and enjoy wine to their heart's content, literally; yet they look great and have a lower incidence of heart disease than we health-conscious Americans. A growing body of medical studies explains that wine—especially red wine—consumed in moderation may be a mitigating factor and is actually good for the heart. We, of course, feel the enjoyment of wine itself is justification enough for its consumption.

So, fellow wine lover, read on for what I hope will be fun, funny, and entertaining. I have written this book for the simple delight of sharing. Let me show you all the different ways we approach wine, as well as where my life and love are centered, and, if you're not careful, you might learn something, too.

January

Feast Days: New Year's Day, St. Vincent's Day

Friday, January 1.   Our year begins and ends with sparkling wine. I can't imagine New Year's Eve or New Year's Day without it, although one thing you should know about me is that if I had my druthers, I would *only* drink sparkling. I panic if we don't have two bottles chilling in the refrigerator at all times. What if something good happens?

I am lucky because we produce seven different cuvées of sparkling. They are very distinct blends, which lets me choose one for every day of the week. Today we had Brut Rosé with a buffet of smoked salmon and bluefish, country pâtés, honey-glazed ham, and homemade breads at Laurence and Terry's house. Laurence says they traditionally pick Brut Rosé for New Year's Day because they like to start the year "in the pink." Last night, we sipped Blancs de Blancs throughout a three-course sit-down dinner at Postrio in San Francisco, which led to dancing on the table, until the restaurant manager politely asked us to step down before we got everyone started. One thing about sparkling wine is that it gives you verve.

Most people do not think of sparkling wine with food. They think of it as an aperitif or an after-dinner drink, something to be enjoyed standing up. I drink sparkling with almost everything. Forrest is used to my predilection; his mother drank only champagne. Her favorite brand was Ayala. At dinner parties, when the red wine was being poured, she would simply ask for champagne and if the host said, "But we're having steak," she'd say, "That's fine."

One of my favorite meals with sparkling is Forrest's roast chicken. Everyone who cooks feels their roast chicken is the best, but Forrest's truly is. He says his secret is the chicken itself. He buys Rocky free range chicken, which is a Sonoma County phenomenon and bears a medal of authenticity like the famous poulet de Bresse. He uses the old Italian trick of putting sliced lemons in the bird's cavity, pushes fresh lemon thyme and lime thyme under the skin, and uses a vertical roaster, which keeps the bird upright so it cooks evenly and makes it much easier to carve. If I'm lucky we eat roast chicken once a week. Plain, it's a blank canvas for just about any wine you can think of. I immediately jump to Blanc de Blancs, especially when Forrest adds a side dish of pasta with a little goat cheese and a drop of Agrumato lemon oil—the lemons are literally crushed with the olives. It goes perfectly with Blanc de Blancs, which is all Chardonnay and so inherently lemony as well.

Generally, I love sparkling wine with everything chicken—from delicious scrambled eggs to chicken soup with Brut, which I think is one of the all-time great food and wine combinations, especially if the carrots, onions, and other vegetables in the soup are fresh and sweet. It's guaranteed to cure whatever ails you.

"Brut" on the label means that the wine is dry. It is typically a blend of Chardonnay and Pinot Noir, which gives the wine an abstract flavor that we think of as a "champagne" taste. The traditional blend is 60 to 70 percent Pinot Noir and the balance Chardonnay. The percentages can vary from vintage to vintage and winery to winery. Brut is rich and creamy, which is the reason it goes so well with clear soup.

The taste and mouth feel of sparkling also seem to respond to ginger and lemongrass. Ironically, it works with everything you can think of that goes with beer—peanuts, popcorn, anything salty, sushi, deep-fried and hot, spicy food, sweet-and-sour dishes, and all the cuisines like Caribbean and Chinese that feature a mélange of different flavors. With stir-fry, for example, the acidity of sparkling does a good job of breaking up all the different flavors in the dish so you can taste the individual components. It's always nice with bread—canapés, gougères (traditional French puffballs of mostly thin air), sandwiches, pizzas, hot dogs, and hamburgers—

because of the yeastiness of the wine. And it's delicious with cotton candy.

One of my favorite dishes with Blanc de Noirs is confit of duck. Another is mushroom risotto. A most memorable meal was one on top of Vail Mountain: grilled portobello mushroom, soft tacos, and Inner Beauty hot sauce with Wedding Cuvée, our Blanc de Noirs. It was snowing lightly and at that high altitude the wine gushed out of the bottle over everything because the pressure outside affects the pressure inside the bottle.

Blanc de Noirs is made from Pinot Noir. It is a purely California creation. Though some French champagnes are made from all Pinot Noir, they do not have the same color. The name literally means white of black (grapes), and therefore technically the wine should have as little color as possible. Nonetheless, we love the pink-gold hue of our Blanc de Noirs and in our winemaking even boost it a little by adding 2 milliliters of Pinot Noir to the dosage to enhance the expectation of Blanc de Noirs—dry like Brut, but more luscious and full-bodied because of the fruit. I remember going around and around on the color with an English wine writer until I finally had to say, "Look. We're not asking for your permission here. Good, bad, or indifferent, this is what we call Blanc de Noirs."

Blanc de Noirs is one of the few sparklings that's delicious with chocolate, provided the chocolate isn't too sweet. It sounds strange that two such favorite tastes could be incompatible, but an overdose of sweetness will point out the dryness of the wine and make it seem tart and austere. Though even this is not the end of the world. The chocolate will taste just fine.

Rosé champagne is one of those categories in which a little bit of knowledge can be dangerous. They are the least understood of all sparklings, though they are usually the most expensive. Many people look at the color and presume the wine will be sweet. Ours is actually the driest of our sparklings and my favorite food with it is steak. I love to serve it in a big burgundy glass—it is primarily Pinot Noir—so you get a bath of bubbles down your throat. It makes me feel like I'm Diamond Jim Brady.

Rosés tend to go in and out of fashion. For the past few years there has been a rather widespread antipathy toward all pink wines as déclassé—too much like "blush wine." King Edward VII favored them, but today British wine expert Michael Broadbent says rosé champagnes are for stage-door Johnnies, which may not be so far off when you think about the Edwardian era. I think they're making a comeback, along with a stab at fun and glamour. Rosés are the most versatile with food. They can carry strong flavors and rich sauces.

In my opinion there's a sparkling match for every dish, as with still wines. All-sparkling menus—where the wines are all bubbly, but in a progression just like still wines—were very fashionable in Edwardian times. Mark has prepared Thai banquets starting with Blanc de Blancs, to Brut, to the fuller richer style of a Blanc de Noirs, then rosé because it is more full-blown, and finishing with Demi-Sec, which is sweet to go with desert. At several dinners we have poured a sparkling throughout the meal as well as a different still to match each course. It shows how a bottle of Brut can carry through to dessert as well as be refreshing at any point in the wine progression. Nothing cleanses the palate quite like champagne.

One of the most interesting all-champagne menus I've ever seen was written by Mark Tarbell and Chef Charles Wiley for the Boulders Resort in Carefree, Arizona.

Extra dry on a label means not as dry as Brut and is an indication of how champagne styles have changed over time. What was once "sec" is now considered sweet. They had to make new names to keep up with the trend. Brut now means dry, though with some dosage. Champagne without any residual sugar at all is called ultra brut, sauvage, natural, or brut zero.

Everything about sparklings should be a lift. I've been told that Napoleon once said that "In victory you deserve it and in defeat you need it." The smell should be floral from the fruit and yeasty like freshly risen bread. The juice itself should be virtually weightless, the most gently pressed. It's not so much that it should be light in body, but that it should capture the light, like a pearl. The texture of the wine should be creamy, which can only come from extended aging. It should effervesce in your mouth, like drinking a cloud. And in the finish, there should be a fillip, a perception of sweetness that is not sugar but an aged characteristic that

CHAMPAGNE ON THE RANGE

May 8, 1992

❖

RECEPTION

Navajo Fry Bread
with Pumpkinseed Cream and Avocado Salsa

Smoked Rock Shrimp
with Jicama and Roasted Pepper Relish

Pan Seared Pheasant
and Grilled Frisee with Lime Sage Aioli

Deutz Brut "Cuvee Lallier"

DINNER

Lobster Tamale with Chipotle Cream
1983 Taittinger Brut

Grilled Mushroom Salad
with Toasted Cumin & Tomato Vinaigrette and Fried Yuca
Krug Grande Cuvee

Smoked Beef Tenderloin
with Singed Onion and Sweet Potato Hash
and a Green Chile Mole
1985 Veuve Clicquot La Grande Dame

Chocolate Cinnamon Torte
with Mexican Brown Sugar Flan
and Caramelized Oranges
Mumm Extra Dry

brings up the wine—and the drinker—in a way that goes beyond the bubbles.

Personally, I see nothing wrong with looking at the world through champagne bubbles, but it can be deceiving. First of all, the bubbles seem to spring from the bottom of the glass as if from nowhere. In fact, they are forming on microscopic particles—proteins and tannins—suspended in the wine. Secondly, you should not judge the effervescence of a sparkling on sight alone. I have tasted champagnes that displayed the most beautiful bead, but the taste of the wine was unappealing, and sometimes a glass that looks completely flat—either because of the glass or because of the temperature of the wine—can have the mouth feel, the softness and creaminess, of perfect bubbles. If it feels like soda water, then the bubbles are too big—what the French call toad's eyes.

The bubbles come from the carbon dioxide created during secondary fermentation and kept under pressure in the bottle. The wisp of cool smoke that first pours out of a freshly opened bottle of champagne is compressed gas. Dissolved CO_2 escapes slowly, ideally rising in a steady stream of perfect, tiny pinpoint bubbles as the pressure is released and the temperature rises in the glass. The size of the bubbles is determined by how carefully the temperature of each bottle is controlled during fermentation and how long the sparkling is aged on the spent yeast cells in the bottle.

There are several theories about the night they invented champagne. Hugh Johnson says English café society, in the time of Charles II, may have "discovered" it. Another rendition comes from a cartoon for the Pacific Wine Company—a well-known San Francisco wine shop, now defunct—which shows a group of monks in a cellar toasting themselves, all saying at once, "Call the attorneys!"

Legally, we can call our wine anything we want in the United States. We are constrained only from saying "Champagne" on labels of bottles shipped to Europe. This puts us in the same boat as fashion designer Yves Saint Laurent, who after months of legal battles was forbidden by the French courts to name a new perfume Champagne. It can be and is called Champagne everywhere in the world except France, Switzerland, and Germany, where it has no name. It became such a marketing coup because of all the free publicity it generated that some people in Champagne suspected it was a calculated move on the designer's part. The latest installment of this story is that Saint Laurent has agreed to drop the name worldwide by 1999, just as we have agreed for export to strike the words *"méthode champenoise,"* which simply means champagne method, i.e., fermented and aged in the bottle. It is the most painstaking, labor-intensive way of making sparkling, a technique to be mastered in the same way that French cooking techniques must be.

As purists, we don't call our sparkling wine champagne for the same reasons we don't call our Pinot Noir Burgundy. We also feel a kind of reverse snobbism. If sparkling is the American name for what we produce, then that's just fine with me. In return, I ask the French to refer to our bottlings as *"les sparklings"* with the proper inflection on the second syllable, spark-*ling.* In French, *vin mousseux* or *vin pétillant* literally means sparkling wine, but has a pejorative connotation as inferior to champagne.

Spanish *cava*, German *sekt*, and Italian *spumante* are technically wines with bubbles, though traditionally made with different grapes. Cava is made from a combination of three grape varieties—Xarello, which provides body, Macabeo for balance, and Parellada, which contributes aroma. The word *cava* for Spanish sparkling wine was coined and made into law at French insistence as a trade issue as recently as 1966. Sekt is 90 percent bulk-produced and made from innocuous white wine grapes often imported from other European countries. Italy's best-known sparkling, Asti Spumante, made from Moscato di Canelli grapes, is sweet. Until very recently French Champagne was more popular in Italy than Spumante, but now—similar to what is happening with sparkling in the United States—that has changed because Ca del Bosco, Bella Vista, and other houses are producing excellent-quality, dry sparkling wine using superior grapes—Chardonnay, Pinot Bianco, Pinot Grigio, and Pinot Nero. Italian producers get around the problem of not being able to use the term *"méthode champenoise"* by calling it *"metodo classico."*

I have long since stopped correcting people about whether they say champagne or sparkling when referring to our wine. I have caught myself saying champagne sometimes because it's easier—people know what I'm talking about, it's familiar, and it's just not a very big issue, except to the French. Technically speaking, champagne is a subset of sparkling.

I certainly don't believe a blind, celibate seventeenth-century monk invented champagne. I think it was Cleopatra. This is strictly my own theory, based on the fact that Dom Pérignon didn't actually discover champagne—the bubbles occurred naturally in the wines of Champagne when the temperatures would start to warm up in the spring, sparking a second fermentation. On the other side of the equation, the ancient Egyptians were sophisticated winemakers. They had vineyard-designated wines. Marked amphora naming the source of the grapes have been found in the tombs of the Pharaohs. The Egyptians had mastered the use of yeast in making leavened bread and beer, and Cleopatra was known to have had every trick of nature at her disposal.

The linchpin of my theory is based on the legend, certainly part fact and part fiction, that Cleopatra made a bet with Marc Antony that she could entertain him in a manner that would exceed the wealth of a nation. The story goes that to win the bet, she took one of her fabled pearls and dissolved it in a glass of wine, which they then drank, but I don't believe that's what happened. I think she seduced him with a glass of sparkling wine. I find it works every time.

January 22. The Feast of St. Vincent. Most occupations have only one patron saint. Wine growers stand out for honoring at least thirty in France alone. There is a preference for martyrs because of the analogy of wine and spilled blood.

Many saints made wine, and the date on which each is honored corresponds to a critical moment in the life cycle of the vine. St. Vincent's Day anticipates the time of renewal. January was traditionally when pruning would start in the vineyards, although now we start in December.

The custom in Burgundy is to decorate the rosebushes and wisteria vines with crepe paper flowers to make them look springlike, even though the weather is cold enough to make you turn blue. There are paper tulips where real tulips are supposed to be, processions with statues of St. Vincent in the lead, and giant, communal feasts.

Unlike Bastille Day and Beaujolais Nouveau Day, we do not celebrate St. Vincent's Day here in California, nor any saint's day for wine. If we had one, I suppose our patron saint would be Fray Junipero Serra. First, though, he would have to be canonized. Father Serra founded twenty-one missions from San Diego to Sonoma. The first clear reference to the planting of grapes in California comes from 1779 in San Juan Capistrano. These vines might have produced a small crop as early as 1781, but historians at the University of California at Davis point to 1782 as the likeliest date for California's first vintage. Their research shows that the impetus for growing grapes and making wine in California was because Spain wasn't shipping enough wine to celebrate Mass.

January 28. I happened to be at my parents' house giving a garden tour—not that there's much to see at this time of year, but gardeners are a strange breed. They don't have to see a plant in bloom to be enthralled.

My parents' house is an old Victorian built in 1876 at the heart of the property, with a big wraparound veranda. Forrest and I live at the foot of the vineyards. We feel we are the gatekeepers. We can hear every car drive by, and to show you how things change, when my parents come home at night, I look at the clock and wonder why they are late.

Laurence, Terry, and their children live at the far opposite corner of the property. It's an old-fashioned way to live. As a friend of ours says, we have kind of a Walton thing going, though the houses are about a quarter of a mile apart, so we do have some degree of privacy.

The garden slopes up from a fruit orchard to long, rectangular flowerbeds and a square terrace where there are dozens of old wine barrels cut in half and planted with herbs. The herb garden is flanked by netted berry patches. Stone steps lined with cutback wisteria lead to a grape arbor and my parents' home. An alternate path to the left goes through the rose garden, also severely pruned, above which more steps lead to a small grassy area, another terrace, the house to the right, and several

acres of hillside devoted to camellias, specimen trees, azaleas, and a collection of rhododendron.

The Big House—as we call it—was falling down
when my parents first moved in. Whatever garden had
been was by then completely subsumed by wild blackberries, which had to be cut out practically with a ma-
chete. My father says he had a plan when he started
carving out the garden but had no idea it was going to
look the way it does today.

His garden is perhaps best understood when it's dormant. The bare-bones design becomes apparent without
foliage, and all the raised stone beds and terraces pop
out in a neat, geometrical way. It is laid out as a series
of rooms or galleries, continuous yet contained, with
leafy walls and doorways. Part of its allure is that it
doesn't show itself all at once. There are several paths to
explore it. Six months from now it will be a near jungle.

The house and the gardens are surrounded by mature
Pinot Noir vineyards now being pruned right alongside
the roses. Forrest planted these vines in 1970 and '71.
He is the one who showed my parents around when
they bought Iron Horse in 1976. That's how Forrest
and I met. My parents sweetly say that first they gave
Forrest the combination to the safe, then the keys to
their cellar, and finally their daughter.

Wandering along the garden paths today, with two
visitors in tow, I got to see our first spring flowers—a
few purple crocuses and a smattering of narcissus-like
white bells, which entitled me to two wishes. We have
a tradition in my family that we can make a wish on

all the firsts—the first of each flower, fruit, and vegetable in season. I can't say if all our wishes come true,
but we certainly get a lot of chances.

We grow all our own produce at Iron Horse. The
vegetables are planted in two main locations—on both
sides of the creek at the entrance to the property and
down by the reservoir, which we call the Lake Garden.
Even in January we have fresh leeks, Brussels sprouts,
beautiful fennel, beets, cabbage, kale, and chicories—
escarole and frisée endive—which this time of year have
a special kind of sweetness because of the cold. In addition, there are the greens grown in flats alongside ferns
and cyclamen in the greenhouse—mâche, arugula, and
Father's personal mix of baby lettuce, known in the
South of France as mesclun, which we cut with scissors
for salad.

Seed catalogs are pouring in for summer vegetables.
In the meantime, the barn where we park the tractors
is filled with winter squash, onions, garlic, potatoes held
in covered bins, and dried hot peppers hanging from
the rafters. There are three freezers crammed with bags
of frozen tomatoes, corn, sweet peppers, and apple
juice, to remind us of the bounty of last year's harvest.

I set today as the start of the new growing season
because of those first flowers at our parents' house,
certainly cause for celebration even though it's winter
weather—cold and wet, and it grows dark at 4 P.M. A
bottle of sparkling wine will go perfectly with a hearty
stew tonight. Champagne originates from a cold climate
and is a staple for the people who grow it.

February

*Feast Days: My Birthday,
Chinese New Year, St. Valentine's
Day, Barrie's Birthday,
President's Day*

February 10. Chinese New Year. This is the Year of the Dog. The first flowering shrub is daphne. Its heady aroma permeates the entire garden. Daphne has elongated leaves and dainty purple flowers, clustered like a natural nosegay. It's a member of the laurel family and consequently a very slow-growing plant. The one by the kitchen door must be at least seventy-five years old and is one of the few signs that there once was a gracious garden at Iron Horse before it was abandoned to the blackberries. In the language of flowers, daphne means glory, though apparently glory is fleeting—this plant gets its fifteen minutes and is rather ordinary-looking the rest of the year. In Greek mythology, Daphne was a nymph who turned into a laurel to elude Apollo.

Daphne is one of my mother's favorite flowers. She

brings whole branches into the house and also fills vase after vase with lovely red quince blossoms. These are the nonfruiting kind. Outside, crocus and grape hyacinths edge the drive and pathways. By the middle of the month, the first daffodils—particularly the early yellow varieties, Dutch Masters and King Alfreds—will take hold. There are thousands in bloom on the hills and surrounding each tree in the orchard. White daffodils—Mount Hoods and Ice Follies—come out later, thickly planted along the ranch roads and in clumps in the cutflower garden. Late in the month, the tulip magnolias and plum trees will come out. There's more and more each day. I swear, if you stand still in the garden, you can watch the buds burst open.

The vineyards, on the other hand, are still completely asleep. There's almost a month's worth of dormancy before their bud break. The day-to-day routine in the vineyards is pruning and tying the canes, which will be the basis of this year's growth, to the trellising wires.

February 12. Today was the kind of absolutely beautiful California day that makes earthquakes seem like a sensible risk: 60 degrees, fresh, blue skies, sailboats on San Francisco Bay. Forrest and I were driving north from San Francisco toward home on Highway 101. The Marin hills were a soft, rolling green carpet, almost as if they had been seeded and mowed. Grazing cattle and the last rays of sunlight on the slopes completed the surprisingly bucolic scene. We turned off Highway 101 and drove west through Sebastopol on 116. The sky was a peach-colored glow to the west and mauve to the east over the Mayacamas. Forrest reminded me that Northern California has a lot to celebrate this year. The winter has been mild. We've had nice rain and the earth didn't open up and swallow our vines (which was to happen due to floods in 1995).

Like all farmers, we feel the full impact of nature every year, not just when it packs a wallop. Each vintage is shaped by the weather. No matter how much Forrest loves us, or how hard he works, he cannot guarantee a great year. It's exactly as Mark Twain said, "The weather is something people talk about all the time, but can't do anything about."

February 14. Valentine's Day is a very different holiday in Sonoma County than in most places. It's a spring holiday here, while it's the dead of winter almost everywhere else.

As on all holidays, Valentine's Day is a chance to make a decision, a commitment—even if it's only to be happy. Forrest and I went on our first date on a Valentine's Day—a champagne and oyster tasting at Hog Island Oyster Farm on Tamales Bay, where we compared Sonoma against France, Oregon, and Washington in both the oysters and the wine. This year, we celebrated with Dean and Lynae Fearing. Dean is the executive chef of The Mansion on Turtle Creek in Dallas and all of Caroline Hunt's hotels. On this occasion, the four of us were on our back deck in shirtsleeves, basking in the sun, and loving fresh, cracked Dungeness crab with bottles of Chardonnay.

Another Valentine's Day, our guests were Charlie Palmer of Aureole Restaurant in New York and Lisa (then) Villarini. My mother had decorated the dining room table with quince blossoms, camellias, and scattered crystal hearts. We had cracked Dungeness crab soup with Wedding Cuvée. Each place setting included an oyster fork as well as a soup spoon, though there was no way to resist diving into the broth with our fingers to try to get at every last bit of crab. Mother had put out her most fanciful china—a nineteenth-century pink Wedgwood, which looks like seashells, ranging from a nautilus sauceboat to outsized clamshell service plates for each of us.

It seemed only natural for us to serve our new release of Wedding Cuvée, even though the bottles weren't labeled yet. Charlie and Lisa made it that much more exciting by announcing plans to elope. Six months later we received a card saying, "Getting tan on Maui and, by the way, we're married."

The crab soup we had is a fairly straightforward French fumet, or fish broth, except that crab is used instead of inexpensive fish. Dungeness crab, unique to the Pacific Coast, can be replaced by blue crab or crayfish.

The recipe involves making a twice-cooked crab broth, meaning that two crabs are sacrificed—cooked until tasteless and then discarded to enrich the broth— then two more are added to the pot. These will actually be served with the dish. This is of course an extremely luxurious way to make crab soup, since Dungeness is 4 dollars a pound even here in California at the height of the season.

That season is from the second Tuesday in November to the end of June, though the crabs are sweetest from February through April. The Department of Fish and Game imposes a strict quota on how many can be harvested, and the price is negotiated between the fishermen and licensed brokers. They in turn sell to wholesalers before the crabs get to the retail market. The fishermen go on strike periodically for more money. Sometimes it's simply not available because of high seas.

Dungeness crab has always been an extravagance. My mother remembers that during the Depression the boat captains paid her father for dental work with crab. He gladly accepted, but learned to insist that the crabs be cracked first. I recommend that you have your fish store clean and crack the crabs.

To make the broth, put one tablespoon of extra virgin olive oil in a large pot, add one diced leek (just the white part), a diced carrot, and a diced celery stalk. Sauté over low heat for fifteen minutes, stirring the vegetables. Add a bay leaf, a small bunch of thyme, two sprigs of parsley, and two of the crabs. Turn up the heat. Cook for another ten minutes. Add six cups of water and one cup of Fumé Blanc. Bring to a boil, then reduce to a simmer and cook for half an hour to concentrate the flavors. Strain the broth, add the remaining two crabs—already cracked—and bring to a boil again. Add a little salt and pepper, and serve the soup hot with chopped parsley or chervil on top. As a first course, this recipe will serve six people.

We like to eat this soup with a simple homemade garlic mayonnaise. Just pound a few cloves of garlic in a mortar, add one egg yolk and a cup of extra virgin olive oil, drop by drop. Using the pestle, work the oil into the yolk until it emulsifies. Add a tablespoon of hot water to the mixture to smooth it out so it's not too pasty.

This crab soup specifies that a cup of Fumé Blanc be added to the broth where most recipes would just say white wine. Fumé Blanc is Sauvignon Blanc or a blend with Sauvignon Blanc as the dominant grape. The name was coined by Robert Mondavi some 30 years ago to distinguish dry, sophisticated Sauvignon Blanc from cheap, sweet jug wine made from the same grape. The confusion began when it became the norm to name premium California wine for the grape varieties. There is still no consensus as to what makes one wine a Fumé and the next a Sauvignon Blanc.

We believe the better the cooking wine the better the dish. Most days there are three or four unfinished bottles on our kitchen counter, giving us a choice of wines to cook with. Leftover white wine holds up for cooking for at least three days and there is always the option of opening up a new bottle, using a bit to cook with, sipping it while preparing dinner, and carrying what's left to the table for the first course.

If you'd rather not, you don't have to use Fumé in

this dish. You could easily use sparkling wine instead. Normally we do not suggest cooking with freshly opened sparkling because it kills the bubbles we work so hard to create, but one cup is not so much to give up, especially when other wines are to follow.

For Valentine's Day, some romantic wines I recommend are: Les Amoureuses, Charlotte's Home from Rodney Strong, and Cuvée Joy. Les Amoureuses is a Pinot Noir vineyard in Burgundy. Charlotte's Home is a Sauvignon Blanc vineyard in Alexander Valley. Cuvée Joy is a wine Forrest named for me. Contrary to what you may think, it's a Chardonnay—a still wine—not a sparkling. It represents one particular section of vineyard. The first vintage of Cuvée Joy was 1990, the year we were married. He wrote a poem to me on the side of the label. It is the only poem I know that contains the word "non-malolactic" (a technical term about changing the acid balance in the wine from malic or apple-like acid into lactic acid, giving the wine a buttery quality often ascribed to Chardonnay), but I feel you should take your poetry however you can get it.

February 20. True to form, the weather went back to winter the day after Valentine's Day. We got six inches of rain over the weekend, with a brief respite today. Forrest and I went hiking around T-bar-T, Forrest's vineyard in the Alexander Valley, for about an hour in the afternoon while the sky was still holding. This is where Forrest spent his summers growing up and where he first planted Cabernet Sauvignon in 1969.

We are pruning in the vineyards as weather permits. You can see where the vineyard workers had to quit last week because of the rain—one row looks as neat and orderly as a line of cadets while the next is a tangle of canes. Bright yellow mustard grows between the vines and little pieces of green Mylar tape flap in the wind against the trellising wires.

We were assailed by the mustard scent as soon as we got out of the truck. It smells a bit like cabbage. The moisture and the warmth of the air really bring it out.

We climbed over one hill of vineyard and down a little valley into the woods. The mustard was replaced by the smell of wet, mulchy leaves. The ground was springy underfoot and abundant with wild chanterelles and huge toadstools. At one time there were signs here that warned "Mushroom Hunters Keep Out!"—which, if I were a mushroom hunter, would have seemed like an irresistible invitation.

The smell changed again at the top of a knoll to wet grass and the first wildflowers—tiny, white fairy bells. On the way back down to the truck, I picked a bouquet of the white bells, a sprig of manzanita blossoms, Spanish moss off the oaks, a bay leaf, and a piece of a mushroom cap and shoved it in Forrest's face. "Doesn't that smell good?" I asked him, to which he said, "It smells like T-bar-T."

By one account, Sonoma is a Patwin Indian word for nose, making this the Land of Chief Nose. The air at Iron Horse is sweet and delicate and utterly intoxicating because of the sheer mass of flowers, especially around my parents' house. At T-bar-T, it's a strong, woodsy, honey smell. The strongest perfume comes from the manzanita blossoms. If you stand in one of the glens surrounded by them, the scent is almost overwhelming. The oaks are also in bloom. Their smell is more subtle, like honeysuckle. Grass has a clean, sweet smell, and at T-bar-T, there's a little wild mint thrown into the mix.

Forrest has a heightened sense of smell, which is crucial for a winemaker. He can discern all the notes in a wine. It's a gift, like having perfect pitch. His nose is extremely sensitive. The downside is that he can be overwhelmed by someone's perfume in an elevator. Once in a café in San Diego, I ordered water with a squeeze of lime, which accidentally sprayed over Forrest's glass of wine, completely screwing up the aromatics of the Chardonnay. Most waiters are baffled when they pour the first sip out of a bottle for Forrest to taste and he just sniffs it, sets the glass down, and nods that it's fine.

For many people, the experience of wine is based primarily on smell. The basic measurable components in wine are sugar, acid, alcohol, and tannin. These elements translate into taste, which the tongue can measure. On top of them are sophisticated "flavors" that we actually smell, like the vanillin or vanilla-like sensation from oak, or the characteristic eucalyptus of Heitz Cabernet from Martha's Vineyard. There is a eucalyptus grove at that particular vineyard, which partially explains or suggests why the smell of the leaves comes through in the Heitz, but it is also because eucalyptus is on the same flavor spectrum as black currant, which is one of the defining characteristics of the Cabernet grape.

Aromatherapists talk about the emotional impact of smells, how vanilla is soothing and lavender is stimulating. We smell roses in Pinot Noir; apples, pears, cinnamon, and nutmeg in Chardonnay. These smells are intoxicating in a way that goes beyond the alcohol in the wine.

Wine is much like perfume. (Perfumers even call their product juice.) Both are mixtures of aromatic constituents and alcohol. When you spray a slip of paper with perfume and wave it around, you're evaporating the alcohol content and carrying the aromatic constituents up to your nose. Swirling the wine in your glass does exactly the same thing.

Flowers vary as much as grapes do. There are seventy-five kinds of lavender. Lavender grown in St. Tropez smells different from lavender grown in the Alps. There can even be vintages of perfume. Some years the fragrance from a particular batch of violets is dramatically more intense than other years, although this distinction is lost mainly because of the large size of most perfumeries. The same is true with wine. Part of what you are paying for in a more expensive wine is vintage variation, those nuances that make one year distinguishable from another, whereas there is a sameness to mass-produced wine.

The smell of crushed violets is said to be erotic. It's a smell that can be very intense in Pinot Noir and in young Cabernet Sauvignon. I can't say whether the sheer smell of a wine will make you feel sexy, but I'm sure that smell alone can give you the sensation of being drunk. Recently we invited two aromatic consultants to Iron Horse. They opened twenty vials of essential oils for us to smell, one after another. Forrest and I both became woozy, then queasy, and ended up with headaches. We couldn't go back to work. We were incapacitated by smell hangovers.

It is very difficult for a wine to redeem itself if the smell is off-putting. No smell at all can mean that the wine is too cold, numbing the taste as well. Smoking is said to kill your sense of smell. Cigarettes and heavy perfume are considered anathemas around wine, at least in California. However, in France all the old cellar masters smoke, just like everyone else.

André Tchelistcheff, one of California's most famous winemakers, who was ninety-two when he died, smoked like a Frenchman until the doctor said no more, but he was always able to mentally filter out the smoke in evaluating wine. Our friend Rob Akins says he was present at tastings at the Jordan Winery where Tchelistcheff would spot and nail vintages he hadn't tasted in ten years. There's also a story that Tchelistcheff tried to stop smoking once before his doctor ordered it, but took it back up because he didn't have time to retrain his senses.

One's sense of smell can be developed. Each of us is born with a certain level of natural ability, which can be augmented to a certain extent with practice. I guess it is aerobic in a way—use it or lose it. My ability to smell has become much more acute since I joined the winery. Even Forrest has remarked on it. I can identify sweet smells like freshly mowed hay, melons, and figs in Sauvignon Blanc, and I can factor out the smell of our dog, Alex, when she's lying under the table in the lab when we're tasting.

Alex herself has a nose for wine. She is a stray who walked onto the property and into Forrest's arms one day. At least, that's what Forrest tells me. I wasn't home. Shortly after she adopted us, we took Alex to the city, where we had a wine tasting to attend at McCormick & Kuletto's in Ghirardelli Square. We parked in the garage, on one of the lower levels, which meant taking an elevator to get to the restaurant. I was standing behind a table, about to pour a taste of our Blanc de Blancs, when I saw our sweet black dog being shooed away at the door. I don't know how she got out—she must have nudged open the back window of Forrest's truck with her nose, and I assume she found us by the smell of the wine.

Sadly, I've heard that the olfactory sense diminishes with age in the same way that a voice loses notes over time, though there are exceptions like the great Mr. Tchelistcheff.

Saturday, February 23, 1991.   AIWF Dinner at the Bel-Air Hotel. The American Institute of Wine and Food was founded by a small group, including Robert Mondavi and Julia Child, to promote fine dining in America.

This particular dinner was a Franco-American event. All of the wines had some kind of transatlantic connection. The Robert Mondavi Winery and Mouton-Rothschild have a joint venture called Opus One, Chalone is in partnership with Château Lafite Rothschild, and we have a joint venture with the Champagne house Laurent-Perrier. The chefs for the evening were George Mehaffey, then at the Bel-Air, and Jacques Pepin, who also painted the menu.

This was a very exciting evening for Forrest and me. We were the first to stand and speak, as Iron Horse and Laurent-Perrier were served up front. Robert Mondavi addressed the Opus One after the main course. He began by talking about us and how we represented the future of California wine. This was my moment in the sun. Robert Mondavi is one of my role models, and I must say he went on at length. Then, at the very end, he said, "Now, I just want to reiterate how exciting it has been for me tonight to see Forrest and Judy. . . ."

Just at the moment when you think you can put your feet up, you can't.

Monday, February 28.   Lunch with wine writer Dan Berger. There were just three of us: Forrest, Dan, and I. Dan was there to interview Mark for an article about winery chefs. The challenge was to display our wine and our chef's talents without one upstaging the other. We served Sonoma rabbit sausage with 1992 Fumé Blanc, pappardelle noodles with Dungeness crab and peas with 1985 Chardonnay, cheeses from Winters, Cal-

AIWF

Menu

Cold and hot Hors d'oeuvre
Iron Horse Blanc de Blanc 86
Laurent Perrier Grand Siècle Magnum 82

Griddled crab cakes with Corn Purée & Fried Pasta
J. Moreau Fils Chablis Domaine Bieville 88

Grilled Leg of Lamb Robert
Beans à la Bretonne

Opus One 87

Cheese and Fruit Medley
Chalone Pinot Noir Reserve 88

Apple - Cranberry Crisp
With Maple - Pecan Ice-Cream
Iron Horse Wedding Cuvée 86
Laurent - Perrier
"Cuvée Alexandra" 82

Chef: George Mahaffey & Jacques Pépin
Bel-Air Hotel. L.A.
February 23, 1991

ifornia, with 1989 Cabernets, and almond pound cake with blood oranges and strawberries for dessert.

Good rabbit is hard to find in most places because so few people eat it. Stores that sell natural meats should be able to order it for you, though it may take a few days' notice. Here in Sonoma, we buy from a lady on Laguna Road, near Joseph Swan Vineyards, whose sign by the side of the road says: CARPETS STEAM CLEANED, FRESH EGGS, RABBITS WITH 24 HOUR NOTICE. Mark stops there to get farm-fresh eggs every day. Of course, chicken, veal, or pork can be substituted for rabbit, and it's not necessary for the sausages to be put in casings. You can simply make patties, as we do in the following recipe.

First bone a two-pound rabbit, cut half a pound of bacon into cubes, and put the rabbit and bacon through a meat grinder using a medium-size plate.

Blend the ground rabbit and bacon with one diced leek sautéd in a tablespoon of unsalted butter and a quarter cup of Fumé Blanc—the same wine being served with the dish. Just use the white part of the leek and sauté it until soft but not brown. Add a quarter cup of fresh bread crumbs soaked in a half cup of heavy cream, and pull the mixture through the meat grinder *twice* to achieve a mousse-like consistency. Add another half cup of heavy cream, one teaspoon of salt, a half teaspoon of fresh grated nutmeg, a half tablespoon of fresh thyme leaves, a quarter teaspoon of ground white pepper, and a quarter teaspoon of cayenne. Mix well and form into patties. Sauté the patties over medium heat for five minutes, flip them over, and sauté on the other side for approximately three to four minutes. You can present them on a bed of arugula with pan drippings.

Forrest chose our Fumé for this dish because Sauvignon Blanc is a very spicy, aromatic grape and therefore goes with aromatic food, showing especially well with the thyme and nutmeg in the sausage. On another occasion, a "Hearts and Dragons" dinner celebrating Valentine's Day, Chinese New Year, and Barbara Tropp and Bart Rhodes's marriage, we thoroughly enjoyed braised rabbit with sage and pancetta and 1978 Robert Mondavi Cabernet Sauvignon Reserve.

March

Feast Days: Justine's Birthday,
St. Patrick's Day, Oscar Night

The spring garden is coming together. There are masses of plum blossoms at the entry to the property. The cherry trees around the main house are so heavily laden that you have to duck under the branches to make your way. Mother loves huge branches of cut blossoms in the house. It is one thing to buy them in a flower market and another to cut them in your own garden where you worry about maintaining the form of the tree. Father therefore planted a far hillside especially for cut blossoms: forsythia, flowering pears, peaches, crab-apple, redbud and, later, lilac. There is a wooden bench on this hill where you can sit with pale, creamy daffodils at your feet, blossoms overhead, and a perfect view of the vineyards—neatly tended, just before bud break—with the Mayacamas Mountains beyond.

The adjacent section of the vineyard is part of the

original planting. They are about twenty-three years old. The trunks are four to five inches around. Forrest is in a race with spring to get the pruning done before the buds push out. This is when the sap rises, when the water sucked up by the roots starts to move up the trunk and into the canes. When you prune the vines, you can feel warm moisture seep out where you make your cuts.

Forrest is also rushing to get the frost protection system running and tested. We have hillside vineyards, so we can't use heaters or wind machines like those you see in orange groves or flatland vineyards. We use six-foot-tall sprinklers planted all over the property to spray water over the vines when the nighttime temperatures drop below freezing. The swirling water creates a warming effect, and the water itself won't freeze as long as we keep it running. We are vulnerable to frost until June, and on a clear night, it is not uncommon to find one of us roaming the vineyards making preparations for frost protection.

Spring is always a jumpy time. The only difference between farming and gardening is that one is our livelihood. I've seen both of the men in my life keep watch after midnight when the threat of frost is at its height or stand by a window looking distraught at rain in late May or early June when the vineyards are in bloom.

March 13. The first Dutch iris appear in the long, rectangular, stone-covered raised beds near the Big House. Dutch iris are my brother's favorite flowers and somehow they must be made to last until his birthday on April 25. By then the flowerbeds will have iris down the middle and crayon-colored ranunculus around the rim.

Father plants new types of iris almost every year — "new this year" color combinations promoted by the catalog companies with exotic names he couldn't resist. German bearded iris outline the rose garden with clumps of violet Japanese iris on slender stems, and low-lying, very delicate wild iris in white and pale sky blue. It's almost like the tulip craze in Holland of the seventeenth century, except that we haven't gone so far as to treat our collection of iris as an investment, which is what happened in Holland and led to a financial collapse. However, Father has at least fifty varieties, ranging from deep purple with the palest of blue and yellow trims, chocolate brown with apricot, mahogany red with pink petals, and one he loves in particular, which is pure chartreuse. Colors never seem to clash in the garden because of the natural iridescence of flowers.

Watercress grows with calla lilies in the marshy area along a narrow creek that carries the runoff through the orchard. We have radishes and baby carrots mixed in with the herbs in half barrels on a terrace leading from the orchard to the Big House. To the right are asparagus planted in long, raised stone beds. This is a damp area. The raised beds protect the plants from rotting. They are lined with wire mesh to keep out gophers.

It takes two years to get an asparagus crop and then, every three or four years, we have to replenish the soil.

For that reason, we have rotating beds, both near the house and down in what we call the Lake Garden, by the reservoir.

We have boundless lettuce—romaine, iceberg, Bibb, limestone, and esoteric French varieties: Quatre Saisons, Merveilles, La Reine de Printemps. I admit we don't worry about waste. With so much abundance, we just eat the hearts.

March 17.   How perfect and perfectly delightful to celebrate St. Patrick's Day with an Irishwoman, Nuala Finn, who was born in Tullow, County Carlow, fifty miles south of Dublin in the Wicklow Mountains and now lives in Puerto Rico where she has a beautiful wine store, Boutique de Vin.

Of all of us, Nuala was the only one not wearing green, though she did have on an Irish sweater. She charmed us with fairy tales and, holding up a glass of Chardonnay, offered a classic Irish toast: "May the road come up to meet you, may the wind always be at your back, and may you arrive in heaven an hour before the devil notices."

Lunch was brisket cooked in ginger broth with fresh baby carrots and steamed potatoes, the last in the barn, served with Chardonnay. Though not specifically an Irish dish, especially because of the ginger, brisket still boils down to meat in a pot with vegetables. Every nationality has this dish, whether it's a New England boiled dinner, corned beef and cabbage, pot-au-feu, or bolito misto. They are all variations on the same theme.

In this case, the aromatics are Asian, making it truly a melting-pot meal.

For a feeling of total self-sufficiency, you might try curing the meat yourself. Put four pounds of beef brisket in a large ceramic or glass bowl, which has been sterilized with boiling water and wiped dry. Pierce the meat with a larding needle, sprinkle evenly with a mixture of six ounces of sea salt and two tablespoons of saltpeter, and scatter a small bunch of fresh thyme and two bay leaves both over and under the meat. You have to then store the meat in the refrigerator for ten to twelve days, turning it every other day.

When ready to cook, rinse the meat in cold water, place it in a medium-sized stockpot, and cover with cold water. Add two small carrots, two large onions halved and stuck with cloves—two in each—and a bouquet garni (twelve parsley stems, eight peppercorns, a quarter pound of fresh ginger smashed, tied in a double thickness of cheesecloth). Bring the water to a boil, then turn it down to a simmer and cook for about three hours.

An hour before the meat is ready, add a sliced turnip, an additional carrot, two celery stalks, a sweet onion (a Walla Walla, Vidalia, or Maui onion) peeled and thinly sliced, a tablespoon of kosher salt, and four ounces of pickled ginger.

When the brisket is done, remove it from the pot, slice the meat on a warm platter, and pour on a couple of ladles of the beef broth. We serve the vegetables—

drained in a colander, but not rinsed — as an accompaniment, with steamed potatoes on the side.

Chardonnay works well with this meal because of the ginger and the sweet vegetables in the broth. No one knows exactly where Chardonnay originated. It may have been growing wild in the central European woods, or it may have been carried north into Europe by Celtic tribes. It was not widely planted in California until very recently. In fact, Chardonnay isn't even mentioned in some of the early California viticultural texts. As late as 1976, when we first came here, there were only 1,481 acres in production in Sonoma County. There are now 55,700 acres statewide.

Chardonnay is the most popular grape in the world, probably because it is so malleable. It can be grown in many different soils and climates, each capable of producing distinctly different styles. It also contains the broadest range of flavors compared to any other grape.

I believe another reason for its universal appeal is that Chardonnay is a beautiful-sounding word. People have used it to name everything from pets to subdivisions. The word has become synonymous with quality.

We tasted our 1993 Chardonnay at our St. Patrick's Day lunch with Nuala Finn. At the time, it was still aging in small oak barrels. Forrest pulled a small sample from the barrel for us to try. It was a green-gold color at this stage, and the fruit and flower components were at their most intense. We talked about the aroma of a young wine versus the bouquet of the new smells that develop with bottle age. This vintage will be bottled in

May and released in September or October, depending on how it tastes and when we run out of 1992.

One of the aspects I love about our Chardonnay is its crisp, green apple character. Part of that is the nature of the grape when grown in a cool climate, but it is also surely because we're located in apple country. All around us are Gravenstein orchards. Green Valley is called the Gravenstein Empire.

The late Eleanor McCrea of Stony Hill Vineyards, one of the pioneers of California wine, wrote that Chardonnay generally is like "green apple, lemon, or citrus, all indicating a fruity flavor and high acid. From extremely ripe fruit come also the descriptions fig-like, pineapple, ripe apples, melon and honey. From the oak of the aging process come the adjectives earthy, toasty, vanilla, caramel, and buttery. Mix them all together and add a distinctive stony edge, known in France as *pierre à fusil,* or gunflint, and you come close to putting on paper a taste and bouquet that can only be hinted at without a bottle in hand."

Forrest adds that our Chardonnay reminds him of taking a stroll through the Casbah because of the spicy smells—clove, cinnamon, and nutmeg.

With wine, the fruit, flowers, vegetables and spices you discern are really all there. Each grape variety has a certain set of characteristics, actual physical, chemical constituents—esters—which can be measured scientifically in a lab with a gastromograph. These esters are the same as the ones found in the fruits and flowers that spring to mind when tasting a wine. Chardonnay has hundreds of constituents, some barely stable, which helps explain why each of us can perceive the same wine so differently.

Each region develops its own vocabulary to describe its wines. According to British wine writer Giles Macdonogh, the names of wild mushrooms are used in Chablis to distinguish various styles of Chardonnay: chanterelles versus mousserons. In Burgundy, cassis, the scent of black currant, in a young red wine means that it is built to last, but if you smell cherries or strawberries they say to drink it up.

Teas, coffees, and perfumes, even single malt Scotches and cigars, are addressed in basically the same language as wine. It is all about nuances, like an art lover discussing different shades of blue, and I'm sure you could translate the attributes that describe a wine into the vocabulary of any other pursuit or area of interest. For example, the "clean" flavors in a wine are analogous to the clean lines in skiing.

There are only four words that strictly define taste—sweet, sour, salty, and bitter. All else has to be simile. We therefore borrow words like "fresh" to describe a young taste and "light" or "big and full" for texture. The British talk about "breeding" being apparent in a wine, what the French call *race,* which means true to type, just as in horses.

"Sweet" is a confusing word. The perception of sweetness can come from fruitiness, alcohol, or the taste of wood barrels, even when the wine has been fermented completely dry and technically there is no residual sugar. One way to tell the difference is whether the wine becomes cloying and makes you thirsty after a few sips. That is often a sign of sugar.

There is no salt in wine. "Sour," or tartness, relates to acidity. "Bitterness" is the result of excessive tannins and comes across in increasing degrees from firm to hard, harsh, coarse, and astringent.

Everyone has different thresholds for perceiving tastes—one person's dry is another person's sweet, in the same way that I can be cold and Forrest can feel like he's roasting in the same room. Part of the beauty of wine is that whatever you taste is all that matters.

Being able to pull the words out of your head to describe your impressions is a matter of experience and associations. It requires a certain playfulness, like discovering figures in the clouds, which, once you see them, seem so obvious even if you can't point them out to someone else.

I admit that the power of suggestion is very strong with wine. If Forrest mentions tropical fruit while we are tasting Chardonnay I will certainly taste it in the next sip.

The way we talk about wine at table is very different from the way we talk about wine in the vineyards or in the winery. Technical talk involves Brix (the measure of sugar at the time of harvest), acid, PH, and yield— how may tons per acre. A winemaker's conversation over Chardonnay might be about how long the wine is left in contact with the skins, which forests they prefer for their barrels, whether to use new oak or old, French or American, light, medium or heavy fire toasting of the barrels, and all the combinations and permutations thereof. "Toast" is part of the process of barrel making that most affects the taste of the wine.

Winemakers talk about malolactic fermentation—a technique that changes the acid balance in the wine, turning malic or tart apple-type acids into lactic or milky acids, and how long the wine is left on the lees (the spent yeast cells)—another technique that contributes to Chardonnay's richness. But *en famille,* when Father asks Forrest what he thinks of a wine that's being served, Forrest picks up his glass, swirls the wine slightly, smells it, and says, "I think it's tasting very good." We don't necessarily go through a sensory analysis of the wine but jump right to our personal conclusions.

"Delicious," or even "yummy," is a perfectly acceptable way to describe wine.

April

Feast Days: Passover, Easter, Earth Day, Laurence's Birthday

Sunday, April 2.   An old quatrain says April is all girlish laughter (sun) followed by girlish tears (rain). Spring rain is different from winter rain. It's more gentle, delicate like filigree compared to hammered silver of winter storms. The greens are vibrant. The place looks electric, like it was plugged in. It's the season for Blanc de Noirs and Sauvignon Blanc. It is also still cool enough to enjoy full-bodied Cabernets, and probably the last time we'll want to drink something so hearty until late fall.

Artichokes require a cool climate like ours. We have half a dozen different varieties and they produce massively every year, making us experts on how to match them with wine. Artichokes make many wines taste sweeter. You should test this for yourself, but we have found that a healthy squeeze of lemon will neutralize the chemical in artichokes that produces this effect. A white wine with naturally lively acidity—Sauvignon Blanc, Sémillon, a cool-climate Chardonnay, sparkling Blanc de Blancs—will accomplish the same result. We serve artichoke hearts and green olives, glistening with lemon juice and olive oil, as an appetizer with Chardonnay. It's surprising to most people, but the artichokes are as much Iron Horse as the wine, so of course they go together.

Our fava beans are even more prolific. You rarely see fava beans in a supermarket. They sell for 2 dollars a pound in the local farmer's market, which leads me to believe we're sitting on a gold mine here, because we have a lot of them. Forrest plants fava beans as a cover crop in the vineyards to feed the soil. Plus, even though it's hard to believe we would want any more, there's another whole plot of favas in the Lake Garden for eating.

Favas grow on tall, leafy stalks, like a big thistle. When they are in bloom, their flowers have two delicate, off-white, rose-shape petals with a deep purple spot, almost like butterfly wings. The blossoms smell like honey and perfume the entire vineyard. The beans grow like Brussels sprouts on the stalks. Like sweet corn, they start to turn to starch as soon as they're picked. They're best very young and tender. Later, they're still delicious, but a nightmare in the kitchen because they take double shelling—first the pod and then the tough outer layer of each bean. We love them simply steamed with a bit of olive oil and chopped fresh herbs, or with shaved dried jack cheese on top accompanied by a glass of Sauvignon Blanc.

Asparagus is also thought to present a problem with wine, but if it is fresh, sweet, and barely cooked, it can be perfect with sparkling, Sauvignon Blanc or Viognier, which tastes like peaches or apricots and is made from a luscious white wine grape traditionally grown in the Rhône valley south of Lyons. Often the problem is the vinaigrette on asparagus because it tends to make wine taste dull. We prefer a drizzle of olive oil and just a drop of lemon or balsamic vinegar, or for hot asparagus, butter or a very light hollandaise.

Generally speaking, Fumé Blanc and Pinot Noir are my favorite wines for spring vegetables. I love Chardonnay or Pinot Noir with mushrooms, except for certain meaty ones like portobellos, which I prefer with Cabernet.

One year, after a particularly rainy February and March, a small cluster of morels suddenly appeared — nine to be exact — poking out of the gravel near my parents' home under a large Douglas fir, which we know from old photographs dates back to the turn of the century. We had them in an exotic ragout, served on toast, which the whole family shared, each of us getting a bite and a glass of Chardonnay.

The value of morels was brought home for Forrest on a mushroom hunt at the Homestead Resort in Virginia last year. The foray was led by Joe Csnarcki, who owned a famous mushroom restaurant in Pennsylvania. Poor Forrest did not find even one and none offered to share, not even our friend Chipp Sandground, who was with Forrest on this trip. Heading back to the hotel, Joe Csnarcki suggested pooling the mushrooms that had been collected for a great stew that he would prepare for everyone to enjoy, but they all refused, clutching their individual bags that much more tightly.

We can buy a variety of exotic mushrooms—shiitakes, portobellos, and blue oyster mushrooms—just down the road from us at the Gourmet Mushroom Farm in Sebastopol. The owner, Malcolm Clark, trades us a bottle of our Cabernet for a pound of his Royal Trumpets, a new mushroom indigenous to the steppes of Asia, which have the nutty, golden taste of porcinis. He mainly sells directly to restaurants, and when we go there we have to maneuver in and out of the driveway between the FedEx and UPS trucks picking up shipments.

April 3. The wines from last year are awakening. We are taking early-maturing wines like Sauvignon Blanc and Viognier out of barrels, assembling the blends, and getting ready for bottling. Once bottling is under way, Forrest and I wake up to the clanking of glass in the morning. The sound rolls down the hill to our house. In fact, we get rattled when we *don't* hear it. Forrest hates it when I say this, because it means that we didn't give the wine any time to settle down, but we were shipping Fumé at the same time we were bottling it.

This is an excellent time for selling wine. The selling season starts slowly in February, peaks in May and

June, drops off during the summer, and hopefully reaches new heights in October, November, and December. I'm on the road most of the spring and fall.

I travel about 50 percent of the time. That's my job. I meet with our distributors, conduct sales meetings, call on accounts — hotels, restaurants, and retailers. My territory is the galaxy. I am scheduled to be in Hawaii at the end of May, Mackinaw Island, Michigan, a week later, and Alaska in June. I feel I should plan a trip to Hilton Head just to complete the picture. The only thing that makes it really seem like work is that I can't be with Forrest. I wish I could be "beamed" everywhere. That way I could come home at night, and I wouldn't need to pack. Those two things alone would make the risk of molecular decomposition worthwhile.

I was born on a Thursday and it is said that Thursday's child has far to go, though I never dreamed that this is what I would be doing. As a teenager, I wanted to be a theoretical mathematician. I applied to Yale as a math major. It seemed so romantic. I had read biographies of several nineteenth-century mathematicians and the most brilliant died very young, either from consumption or in duels. They were like poets, always seeking the simplest, most elegant answer to problems.

I backslid into history and economics and graduated wanting to be Woodward and Bernstein. In the early eighties, I aspired to be president of ABC News.

Now my dream is to live at Iron Horse and sell lots of wine. So, you tell me, is it totally strange or all too predictable that I found my calling within the family fold?

Our problem in the wine business is an embarrassment of riches. A very fine wine list in a restaurant might offer a full page of Chardonnays, say, thirty-five selections, but that's out of the thousands made around the world. There are at least 800 Chardonnays from California alone. In the face of so much competition, my marketing philosophy is "down with the ship." We will sink or thrive on the quality and individuality of our wines.

There are as many theories on selling wine as there are on making it. In Chicago this month I heard about one of our confreres, who comes in once a year—five people from the winery for a five-day blitz of tastings, sales calls, and incentive programs. They sell a thousand cases in one week in one city and then move on. Our philosophy is to have continuity in each market, so we slug it out month by month. After ten years with the winery, I still haven't found any magic ways to sell wine except one account at a time.

I frequently pour at consumer tastings. If I could, I would talk about our wines with every American of legal drinking age. I recently trotted out the newly labeled Wedding Cuvée at a consumer tasting in southern California. This was the first time anyone had tasted this vintage outside the winery. One gentleman at the tasting clearly did not like the new release. He made a terrible face and walked away from the table. Then he came back and offered to tell me what we were doing wrong. He said, "There's too much cuvée in your wine. If you used a little less cuvée it would be better." Not everybody, as you can tell, knows what cuvée means. It means blend. It can also refer to a particular lot or batch of wine, representing a section of vineyard or a particular cut of the juice as it comes out of the press. Most people think of cuvée with regard to sparkling, but it is also used for Chardonnays, and the phrase *tête de cuvée* was once used in Burgundy to indicate the best of the vintage.

Much of selling wine has become programming— short-term deals usually lasting sixty to ninety days to capture the imagination of the distributors as well as the customers. An example would be a discount on Chardonnay for on-premise—hotels and restaurants— who commit to twenty-five cases that can cum (accumulate) over a two-month calendar period. Programs tend to be advertised on a special sales sheet or on the front page of the distributor's monthly price book, which theoretically would have the additional effect of at least putting the words Iron Horse in front of customers whether the salesperson mentions us or not. There is an art to programming, but once you get on that road, it is very difficult to get off. It becomes a built-in cost, effectively a price cut, unless you raise prices to pay for the programming.

My basic sales technique is kiss and beg. The most remarkable aspect of my sales meetings is that I offer little more than our wines. My personal theory on incentives is that virtue should be its own reward—that and the chance to make percentage.

My only real concern is why both my husband and my father keep planting more vineyard. I have accused them of not loving me because the more wine we make, the more I will be out on the road.

April 10.   Forrest is immersed in a new growing season. The first round of disking and mowing in the vineyard is under way. This is also when new vineyards are planted.

There's still a fair amount to be done to make up for phylloxera, a vine louse that wiped out most of the world's vineyards beginning in the southern Rhône valley in 1867. Ten years later the vineyards of Bordeaux, Burgundy, and Champagne were dead or dying. It struck in Austria-Hungary in 1872. A few years later it had reached Switzerland, the Rhine, and the Moselle, then Madeira, Spain, and Portugal. Italy tried to escape, enacting legislation against the import of vines, but was invaded in 1875. By 1880 the vineyards of South Australia were ravaged. Four years later South Africa's vines capitulated. Algeria was the next to fall. In 1890—some say earlier—phylloxera swept the California vineyards.

Phylloxera's return or mutation was discovered in Napa and Sonoma almost on the centenary of the last scourge. No antidote has been found. The only recourse is to uproot infested vineyards and replant on what we hope is resistant rootstock.

Forrest has pulled out 40 acres at T-bar-T and replanted 37. He will replant the remaining 3 this year. We have about 8 acres still to go, which Forrest plans to pull out this fall, after the harvest, or next year depending upon how fast the phylloxera spreads in that block. If it spreads slowly we'll be able to keep this section in production one more year. It is merely delaying the inevitable, but right at the moment the market is very good—there's a need for Cabernet—overall production is down because of phylloxera and prices are high. If it's possible, it would behoove us to bring in some cash from T-bar-T instead of only *spending* money on it at the rate of $10,000 an acre.

We hit the low point in terms of crop size in 1993— though those wines won't hit the marketplace for several years. We made 2,400 cases of Cabernets in '93 compared to 4,000 cases in '90, our current release. Now, hopefully, production is going back up. This year should be substantially more than last, all else being equal. Then, when those eight acres are pulled out, once again production will go down by 24 tons—about 1,500 cases—a significant swing in our marketing.

Phylloxera has caused many vintners to switch varietals in certain areas. This is said to be the silver lining, because it should result in better wines. This April or May, Forrest will plant three acres of Sauvignon Blanc where Cabernet Franc used to be, because that section did not yield the best Cabernet Franc. Perhaps a different grape will do better. In the short term, styles of wine will change from those wineries that had to replant because wines from young vineyards simply taste different.

The remaining 8 acres of Cabernet Sauvignon, once pulled out, could also be replanted as Sauvignon Blanc, balancing all the Viognier—14 acres to date—and bringing our Fumé Blanc production as high as 7,000 cases by 1999.

While he's at it, Forrest is developing a new piece of land, which will be planted to Cabernet Sauvignon. It's 5.5 acres, 1,000 feet off the valley floor on a 30-degree-angle, west-facing slope. Forrest has not had a vineyard there before. It's a parcel he tacked on while he was replanting anyway. This was a little bit difficult for him to justify. "I see it as long-term insanity," he says, "moving forward in my dream of having more vineyard at T-bar-T."

What has phylloxera meant to the marketplace? It means that 7,000 acres in Napa alone are not producing grapes this year. That's a major shortage—a 70-million-dollar hit to the industry right there.

The concomitant increase in the value of grapes is such that Forrest could sell half his 1992 Cabernet production on the bulk market at 13 dollars a gallon and pay for the entire cost of bottling the rest. The pressure would be on him to make a great 2,500 cases to warrant the decrease in production, which means deciding at this early stage what lots he would want to keep and which ones he would be willing to sell eighteen months before we'd be ready to release this product on the market. Predetermining our blend, what will be bottled as Iron Horse wine, involves taking down all the barrels and tasting each one at the same time that we are racing to finish pruning, bottling Fumé Blanc, and labeling more sparkling before Easter. It turns out that not selling grapes is as luxurious for a winemaker as not buying any.

Fortunately we are phylloxera free in Green Valley, both because of our soil type and because the vineyard was planted to an old-fashioned rootstock that isn't susceptible. Iron Horse has *"vielles vignes,"* as the prephylloxera vines in France are called.

April 15. April is a time of ritual—the rites of spring in the garden and the traditions of Passover and Easter in the home. Passover and Easter are seldom more than days apart. They share the same flowers, the tradition of family feasts, and the tradition of wine. The Last Supper was a Seder. Christ took a cup in his hands, blessed it and gave it to his disciples, saying: "Drink ye, all of it, for this is my blood."

We celebrate both Passover and Easter. My family is Jewish, Terry is Catholic, and Forrest was raised Episcopalian. We all share the feeling that this month celebrates the bursting of the new year. It's the time of bud break in the vineyard. The dining room table is decorated with plain white eggs mixed with the first pastel rosebuds in ornate, cut-crystal bowls.

Starting in March but now in full swing is Father's system of rotating plants on the verandas and terraces around the house. Pots of pansies and cyclamen are replaced with daffodils. Gradually pots of tulips are phased in, predominantly white; pale, creamy yellow;

and deep maroon—about twelve varieties, to get as long a run as possible. Some are tall and slender like Queen of the Night. The ones with ruffled petals are called parrot tulips. There are also pots of white and blue hyacinths strategically placed near the front door to perfume the steps as you enter the house. There's a saying that no matter how poor you are, half your money should go to food and the rest for hyacinths to feed the soul.

The lilac comes in white, blue, and strong purple. In the house, large vases are filled with bouquets, the colors changing from room to room. The cut tulips come in all shades. They grow in a big square bed, lined with metal mesh, on the far side of the berries, near the calla lilies and watercress. They will get pulled out in June and the bulbs stored in bags in a cold, dark wine warehouse until December replanting, freeing up the bed for dahlias. A trick that keeps cut tulips alive for more than a few days in a vase is to drop a piece of copper in the water with the flowers. This tradition started in England using pence, but since the American penny has hardly any copper content, my mother uses scrap from replaced drain pipes.

I have promised myself I will not miss a single spring flower this year, including the wildflowers. In the meadow around our house we already have lupine from the seeds I gave Forrest for Valentine's Day last year, crimson clover, scarlet maids, and some California poppies just beginning. At T-bar-T there are whole hills blue with lupine. We lie down for an hour in the afternoon in a field of forget-me-nots, buttercups, purplish wild phlox, and something magenta and tufted that smells like clove.

My father leads our Passover Seder. His ceremony is somewhat truncated, but traditional. We pour off spoonfuls of red wine from crystal glasses as a sacrifice to ward off plague, pestilence, and all other evils. We make special blessings and give thanks to God for bringing forth the fruit of the vine. We pour a goblet of wine for the prophet Elijah and open the door of our home to any stranger who might have need.

Our Passover menu this year was carciofi alla Giuda—deep-fried artichokes—with 1989 Blanc de Blancs; cold poached black bass with vegetable relish and 1992 Chardonnay; lamb shanks with 1983 Cabernet Sauvignon in magnums; and chocolate-bottomed coconut macaroons.

Passover to me means red wine. We drank 1983 Cabernet during the ceremony and then went back to it with the lamb shanks. The fried artichokes is an old Roman-Jewish recipe. It's perfect for baby artichokes, which haven't yet formed actual chokes, and so can be simply cut in half with an inch or two of the sweet, young stem. We figure four per person as an appetizer.

First, trim the tops of the artichokes and peel off the outer leaves as well as the outer layer of skin on the stems, then cut them in half. A squeeze of fresh lemon juice on the cut halves prevents them from browning as they are drying on a paper towel.

Heat 2 cups extra virgin olive oil and 2 cups canola

oil in a frying pan to 300 degrees. Place the cut artichokes in the oil for approximately three minutes to
begin the cooking process, then remove them with a
slotted spoon to a rack or a tray covered in paper towels
to drain excess oil. Heat the oil to 350 degrees and add
the artichokes. Sauté until they are golden brown.
Again remove them from the pan and blot with paper
towels to remove excess oil. Sprinkle lightly with salt
and pepper and add a little lemon juice to taste. The
squeeze of lemon at the end makes the dish compatible
with wine, especially one with acidity like sparkling.

The centerpiece of our Easter meal is ham, which we
traditionally serve with Brut Rosé because Easter is a
celebration and calls for sparkling. The colors of the
rosé and the ham are gorgeous together, and the bubbles magnify the essence of the spices in the ham—the
juniper, nutmeg, and vanilla. A red wine might seem
tart or bitter.

Home-Cured Easter Ham

It will take two weeks to make this ham. It involves
many small steps. The most important is keeping everything very clean.

Serves 8

Ingredients:
1 18-pound hindquarter of fresh ham with the bone
   removed
2½ pounds sea salt

¼ pound brown sugar
1¾ ounces saltpeter
parchment paper
2 quarts cold water
4 bay leaves
small bunch of thyme
3 dozen peppercorns
3 dozen coriander seeds
12 juniper berries
4 vanilla beans, split lengthwise
1 head nutmeg, crushed
honey for brushing

Directions:

Mix a half pound of sea salt with the brown sugar and saltpeter in a sterilized stainless-steel or glass bowl. On a very clean table, place the ham skin side down and massage evenly with the salting mixture. Turn over and do the same on the other side. It is very important to rub this mixture in evenly and thoroughly for a nice pink color.

Sterilize an earthenware container large enough to hold the ham. Place ham skin side down. Cover with one pound of sea salt and protect with parchment papers. Let stand two days. Then, turn the ham using a sterilized meat fork—*never touch the ham with your fingers.* Cover this side with remaining pound of sea salt and new parchment papers. Let stand for another two days.

To make the brine, remove the ham, place on a sterilized tray, and put aside in a cool place. Empty the remaining contents from the earthenware container into a large saucepan, add cold water, bay leaves, thyme, peppercorns, coriander seeds, juniper berries, vanilla beans and nutmeg. Bring these ingredients to a boil, boil for 3 minutes, remove from heat, and let cool.

Return the ham to the earthenware container and pour the brine over the ham, covering it. Turn the ham every two days, or every day if it is not completely immersed in the brine. The ham will be cured in ten days.

Remove the ham, rinse under cold water, place in a large braising pan, and cover with cold water. Bring water to a boil, then reduce to a simmer. Poach the ham at 175 degrees, allowing twenty minutes per pound.

Let the ham cool in the poaching broth, then transfer it to a sheet tray. Brush with honey and place under a broiler to caramelize.

Remove from the oven, slice, and serve.

Just as there are rituals of cooking and eating, there is a whole canon surrounding how wines should be handled and enjoyed: breathing, decanting, and temperature; the ritual of tasting wine in a restaurant before it is served; cork sniffing and swirling, as well as the manners of tasting wine in a winery, like spitting. Most of the customs and conventions of wine drinking are matters of trial and error. They are not rules but something to be verified for oneself. Some do not seem to have any rational explanation, or if they did, it has been lost in the mists of time.

For example, according to custom, a port decanter should be passed from left to right. One theory is that it goes back to the time of the Druids and follows the movement of the sun. Another is that passing the port from the left means it is heartfelt.

It is also customary to open a bottle of red wine to let it breathe before serving, which in reality does very little, unless you pour the wine into glasses, because hardly any air actually gets to the wine while it's in the bottle. Oxidation is part of how a wine ages, and some experts recommend decanting young vintages, not because there's any sediment but on the theory that aeration will help the wine open up and soften. For the same reason, we advise waiting until the last minute to decant older wines lest they fade before we get to them.

The punt or indentation on a still wine bottle is obsolete and purely esthetic. It's where hand-blown glass was originally secured on a rod while the bottle was spun and blown from the neck. On a champagne bottle, however, the punt adds to the strength of the bottle so it can withstand the six atmospheres of pressure generated by the second fermentation. A deep indentation also makes it easier to stack inverted champagne bottles one on top of the other while they are aging at the winery.

It is considered poor service to make a loud noise in opening a bottle of sparkling. You are supposed to hear only a sigh, which I guess is a sign of control, like an Olympic diver who enters the water without a splash, but I think it's too bad. We spend so much time, effort, and money building up that pressure inside the bottle that I like to hear a big pop. I think it's one of the most fun sounds in the world.

Only once have I seen someone stick a thermometer in his glass to take a wine's temperature, an act that struck me as entirely affected. A wine served too cold will take care of itself with time. One that's too warm can be chilled in a bucket of half ice and half water — about twenty minutes for sparkling and ten or fifteen for Chardonnay. The neck of the bottle is always the last to cool down. My solution is usually to pour just a few sips into everyone's glass, then put the bottle on ice and keep pouring out small amounts until the bottle is cold. We don't make it a practice, but I have seen Forrest add ice cubes to a glass of Chardonnay, which brings down the temperature but dilutes the wine. All red wines, even the most expensive, deserve to be chilled on a hot day — just set on ice for five or ten minutes.

I happen to be very fussy about corks. To me the quality of the cork in the bottle speaks of the quality of the wine. I truly enjoy looking at them, like a gemologist giving more than a passing glance to a stone. When someone passes me a good cork, I willingly admire it.

Not every vintner feels this way. In an effort to demystify wine, Michael Mondavi on more than one occasion when handed a cork in a restaurant has been known to say, "I never know what to do with these things," then pop it in his mouth and start chewing on it, to everyone's disbelief.

Cork is controversial within the wine world because even low-end, never-to-be-aged wines are now cork finished purely for marketing reasons. As a result, cork has become very expensive—top-grade, hand-sorted, air-dried natural cork from Spain or Portugal costs 30 cents apiece, and there is some argument whether it does anything—whether enough air really gets through the cork to significantly contribute to the aging of the wine.

The ideal cork is supposed to be long, perfectly smooth, and very tightly grained, without cracks or perforations. It should be odorless in a young wine and the tip should be barely wet.

The cork is just a stopper. Some wineries use synthetic closures, which look gorgeous and provide a perfect seal, but we feel the tradition of cork has yet to be improved upon because of how it naturally changes with time. The cork from a very old bottle is truly something to behold. We recently opened a forty-year-old Bordeaux whose cork was wet and mushroomy, quite sensual actually, and begged the question whether its rich, earthy smell came from the wine or vice versa. It was a conversation we enjoyed immensely.

Swirling is a time-honored tradition among wine lovers. It releases the aromatics of a wine and is the reason you don't want the glass more than half filled. Spitting is something I never do in public. I'm too afraid of dribbling wine down my front. I do adhere to the custom of clinking glasses. One theory about how clinking started is that it sounds like church bells and wards off the devil. Another is that wine involves four of the five senses, and touching glasses brings in sound. Certainly it is a gesture that includes everyone in an occasion, and as a friend of mine says, "Nobody wants to be the missing clink."

Monday, April 18. Picnic at T-bar-T. There's something very special about drinking wines in their birthplace: the trees, the lay of the land, the nature of the soil, the feeling of the air, a blue heron on the reservoir. Each vineyard has its own quirky confluence of elements that make it special for growing grapes. The concept of *terroir* includes how the land is tended, how the vines are staked in relation to the sun or slope, and how the vintner interpreted the land. The way the wind blows is as important to a vintner as it is to a sailor. At T-bar-T, a northwesterly wind usually comes howling through this narrow corner of Alexander Valley at 35 miles an hour in April or May and can dry everything out so that the hills change from green to gold practically overnight.

We learn which grapes to grow through trial and error. Robert Louis Stevenson wrote about this during his honeymoon in California in 1880, in *Silverado Squatters* when Napa, just one ridge over from T-bar-T, was still "a land of stagedrivers and highwaymen." Winegrowing was in its experimental stages. He wrote: "The beginning of vine planting is like the beginning of mining for precious metals. The wine grower also 'pros-

pects.' One corner of land after another is tried with
one kind of a grape after another. This is a failure; that
is better; a third best. . . . The smack of California earth
shall linger on the palate of your grandson."
We are still evolving. Forrest has planted the traditional grapes of Bordeaux, Tuscany, the Loire, and the
Rhône valley at T-bar-T. He blends Cabernet Sauvignon and Cabernet Franc into a proprietary red we call
"Cabernets." He is experimenting with Sangiovese and
Merlot like the developers of the so-called Super Tuscan wines, as well as Sauvignon Blanc and Viognier,
which shows he has completely lost his mind. Sauvignon Blanc originates from the Loire and Bordeaux; Viognier from the Rhône. These two regions would never
comingle their grapes. It would take a Californian to
blend them. Perhaps that is part of the nature and ex-
citement of California wine, that we are always
experimenting.

The picnic ground at T-bar-T is almost at the top of
the property, about 700 feet above the valley floor. It
feels like the top of the world. The view from here
is wide and commanding, about 150 degrees, looking
southwest across the river to the thin wisps of fog almost directly over Iron Horse. There's an old redwood
picnic table with a few tree stumps set around it for
chairs, surrounded by clumps of wild iris that rise above
baby-blue-eyes and yellow meadow foam. It was a very
warm day. We could sense summer just around the
corner.

We bring real glasses with us on picnics, but only

one glass each, to lessen the load, so when we want to switch from one wine to the next we simply throw anything left in the glass on the ground. "From dust to dust," said one friend.

Lunch was cold asparagus vinaigrette; roast chicken and polenta; salad; cheese; and bread. We drank very young wines, all grown at T-bar-T: 1992 Fumé, barrel samples of Sauvignon Blanc, and Viognier from 1993, 1990 Cabernets, and the individual components from the successive vintage—barrel samples of 1991 Cabernet Sauvignon, Cabernet Franc, Sangiovese, and Merlot. We made a trial blend of these last barrel samples right there in the middle of the vineyards. "The ultimate field blend," said Forrest, pouring a dollop of each variety into a glass. Young reds are typically vibrant and angular. They usually have a hard edge that will smooth out with time, but the samples we had with us showed an intrinsic softness that is one of the defining elements of the Alexander Valley. What that means, translating the winespeak, is that Alexander Valley on the label means the wine inside is typically good early drinking.

I mentioned my experiment of picking fragrance bouquets at T-bar-T at least once a month to see if the smells throughout the year relate to the wine and was quickly reminded that in the old days farmers used to eat dirt to taste the Ph in the soil, and even that was one-upped by the story about a French winemaker who, to learn his vineyard in Napa, stripped off his clothes and rolled on the ground naked to get a feel for the land.

April 22.   Earth Day. In front of the Big House, one of the most spectacular shows is a large white fringe tree (Chionanthus), below which are masses of snowballs. Carrying the white theme around to the south side of the house are Portuguese laurels with long, graceful white blossoms and Pieris japonicas, called lily of the valley trees because of their cascading bell-shaped flowers. There is also a large flowering pear, which you can see from the library. In its early years this pear refused to bloom until Father gave it an ultimatum, threatening to chop it down if it didn't perform, which must have scared the tree because it has bloomed magnificently ever since.

The whites in the garden seem to glow at dusk, like a moon garden. There's a short loop we like to take, glass of sparkling in hand, before dinner, off the terrace and up some stone steps past the camellias to another set of stairs, where a philadelphus adds its masses of white blossoms in an archway you have to duck under to continue up the hill. Philadelphus is also called mock orange because the flowers look and smell like orange blossoms. "There's something about a glass of sparkling that seems to go with the colors and smells of the garden," says Father.

The camellias at my parents' house stand 8 feet tall and are covered with masses of blooms. Some of the white ones are so perfect they could have been the prototype for Coco Chanel's signature white silk camellia pin. There's a bleeding heart halfway up the hill. It's a low plant with long, curved stems and small pink and red flowers hanging down that look like crying hearts, hearts with a teardrop on the end, which remind me of a Salvador Dalí. Climbing up one of the tall trees is a vanilla-scented clematis vine reaching for the light. Father's plan is to plant more of them to spiral up his corkscrew willows and ginkgos.

The path leads to rhododendron and azaleas, exotic ferns, calla lilies, a moss-covered stone grotto, then across a small wooden bridge to the cut-blossom garden and down a set of railway ties used as stairs, with lilac on your left and vineyard on your right. To get back into the garden, there's a small fence, ostensibly to keep out deer, and a large white rock from the mother lode area in the Sierras, which sits like a sculpture behind a small garden bench with another philadelphus overhead. This is the way back to the dining room.

We sat down to the first course of a rich, opulent meal—clear lobster soup with plump pink pieces of lobster, black truffles, ginger, and spring vegetables— served with Brut Rosé. The main course was rack of veal with turnips, onions, and porcini mushrooms and 1988 Pinot Noir—a light vintage, which is what we wanted in order not to overpower the veal. An older, more substantial Chardonnay could have been an alternative, such as Corton-Charlemagne from Burgundy or a Chalone from California. These are matches based

more on the texture and weight of the food and the
wine than on a specific taste. We then had garden lettuce with sheep's milk pecorino pepato studded with
whole peppercorns, and 1983 Cabernet Sauvignon, followed by strawberry semifreddo with Demi-Sec for
dessert.

May

*Feast Days: May Day,
Mother's Birthday, Cinco de Mayo,
Mother's Day, Memorial Day*

Sunday, May 1. By now the vines are growing very rapidly. They still look orderly and trim, like dancers, arms outstretched, sashaying up and down the hills. The young leaves are vibrant green-gold.

In the winery, we are topping off barrels of young wine. Having released our new vintages of Fumé Blanc and Wedding Cuvée, we focus now on 1991 reds, which are ready to come out of barrels. Forrest and his assistant still winemaker taste all of the lots one by one and then in every conceivable combination.

There are twenty-eight batches. Each represents a different section of vineyard, particular press runs, and four types of oak barrels. The split between the different grapes is about 60 percent Cabernet Sauvignon and 40 percent Cabernet Franc.

Each lot is a piece of a puzzle with no preordained

picture to achieve at the end. Ironically, all the favorites mixed together do not necessarily make the best wine. Some, which by themselves taste incomplete, may be important components of a blend. Others are needed to provide a smooth transition from taste A to taste B, and not everything always fits into one bottling. It is easier for me as the marketeer if we end up with only one master blend, but there are so many variables and no formula for how they will come together. The final decisions can only be made on taste, and given the same components I bet no two winemakers would produce identical blends, just as photographers shooting the same scene will yield very different images.

In terms of the garden in May, Father's crucial item of concern is the timing of the lilies of the valley. He plants the bulbs in stages in a series of small pots, aiming to have them bloom on May Day for the five ladies in his life and on May 5, Mother's birthday. This sounds simple, but lilies of the valley do not always cooperate. Sometimes the bulbs advance too fast. If they start to sprout in the bags before the scheduled planting time they will become too leggy. Or they can be impossibly slow growers. To be certain of success, Father triples what he needs. In Paris, you can buy lilies of the valley in cut bunches on street corners. Growing them at home is far more challenging and therefore, I can say, even more appreciated.

This May Day we celebrated my great-uncle's ninety-fifth birthday. It was an important occasion for Mother as a milestone in our lives and because her whole side of the family was here.

The menu included our chef's signature dish, grilled quail skewered on grape vine canes with tamarind glaze. It's one of those recipes that begins: "First, gather a bundle of vine cane cuttings from the vineyard. . . ." The canes are soaked in water overnight so they don't burn on the grill. They don't impart that much flavor to the quail, but it's fun to do because we're a winery and we love to use what we have on the property. Olive or rosemary branches can be substituted as skewers. Grape vines burn very hot, so we use them as kindling to start the fire for grilling and then usually add oak, alder, or apple wood, which we also have in abundance. We served Pinot Noir, which is a classic combination with quail because of texture and weight and because Pinot Noir is a natural with smoky flavors.

The quail come from Bud Hoffman in the Central Valley, around Stockton. His are an ounce or two larger and more flavorful than the standard-size quail from the big commercial farms. They also bear no resemblance to the sweet little birds that scatter across the ranch roads at Iron Horse.

Place the quail in a bowl and toss with olive oil, salt, and pepper. Skewer the quail, inserting the cane through the cavity of each bird, positioning the quail in the center of the grape cane, and secure it with a 12-inch length of butcher twine tied at the drumstick and at the wing, snipping off any excess string.

To make the glaze, sauté two tablespoons of minced

garlic, two tablespoons of minced shallots, and two tablespoons of minced ginger in two tablespoons of peanut oil for two to three minutes, then set aside. Combine
three tablespoons of palm sugar and three tablespoons
of fish sauce in a small saucepan, and cook over medium
heat until caramelized. Add a half cup of water, three
tablespoons of tamarind paste mixed with three tablespoons of water and six tablespoons of lime juice. Reduce this mixture by a third. Add the sautéd garlic,
shallot, and ginger.

The next step is to prepare a wood fire and grill the
quail over hot coals for twelve to fifteen minutes, turning the quail every few minutes and brushing with
the glaze.

To serve this dish, we leave the quail on the grape
vine cane and eat them the way we would corn on the
cob. Eight quail will serve four people as a main course
or eight people as an appetizer. We have discovered
that if you present the quail on a platter people will
take one each, but if you put two on their plate they'll
eat both.

Uncle Sam's main ambition is to live to see three
centuries. I'm sure he'll do it. It's what keeps him going.
After his birthday lunch, Uncle Sam made a toast in
which he said, "Life has its ups and downs. My advice
is to stay busy and be happy." It's as simple as that.
Happiness is a choice we get to make in life. But no
matter how old or wise you become, everyone feels the
same about aging. A week later, looking at the photographs from his birthday party, Uncle Sam became very

upset. "Oh, my God," he complained, "I look like I'm a hundred and ten."

May 5. Mother's birthday. My parents' house is encircled by trees, some hundreds of years old. We have lost a few of the oldest ones, which, though heartbreaking at the time, has allowed the trees my parents planted to grow and assume their place in the garden. I lose count of how many shades of green there are among these trees. This month, the Japanese maples are leafing out, adding their bronzes and reds. There is also a copper beech and three tricolored beeches—pink, green, and cream—which were a gift to my parents from Grandma Sara, my father's mother. They are very slow-growing trees, but the translucent colors when the sun shines through the leaves make the wait worthwhile.

The idea of mixing all kinds of tree colors and forms comes from the Imperial Gardens outside the Japanese summer palace in Nikko. There is a saying, "See Nikko and die," because of its extraordinary beauty. My parents were most impressed by the vast array of trees with all their different colors and textures, which the Emperor had had planted to be a special source of pleasure when he looked out from his bedroom window.

For my parents, some of their most satisfying moments take place in a glass alcove, an extension of the dining room where they usually enjoy their wine and lunch—rain or shine—while gazing at an ever-changing view of trees and potted plants arranged along the garden wall. This morning, Father brought out several tree peonies in pots, which he placed in the prize location in front of the alcove window to be on view during their few days of glory. There are six or seven clear glass bud vases on the table, each one holding a different-colored rose—the first of the season.

My parents sit down to lunch at one o'clock. Early May surely means fava beans—we have fava beans one way or another with every meal this time of year. Mark is likely to have prepared something exotic like grilled boar sausage with braised onions to go with Cabernets and soufflé pancakes with cream and caramel sauce for dessert. The menu is the same for the two of them as it would be for guests, for whether they are at a banquet or just having a salad and a glass of Pinot Noir, my parents' pleasure in dining is a cornerstone of what they consider the good life.

I come from a long line of people who believe life is meant to be enjoyed. I inherited that gene from both my parents. I think they have always been motivated by how they want to live. That's why we moved to France in 1967 and that's what brought us to Iron Horse in 1976.

I recently asked my mother what she thought about hedonism and she said, "I guess it's all right, as long as you can afford it and you aren't hurting yourself or anyone else," though she said she wouldn't call any of us hedonists, because we work hard.

My mother preaches moderation. "Even water," she says. "If I drank too much water, I'd drown." I always tease her by asking if she includes moderation in moderation—meaning that some kind of blowout would be necessary every once in a while, but she sticks to her guns.

Her personal style is *"abbondanza."* Ask her what it means and you get this: "You know . . ." with a full, generous sweep of her hand in the air. She is not Italian. I should ask her where she got the term, but I interpret it to mean spilling over with quality—lavish, but comfortable, like the massive bouquets of peonies she cuts from the garden. Below the roses and bounded on the other side by a small boule court is a cutting garden filled with daffs, Icelandic poppies, anemones, and ranunculus surrounding a variegated box elder tree; there's a whole section for pink and white peonies.

Somehow, Mother reconciles *abbondanza* with her preaching of moderation. "It's just an appearance," she says. "I notice that everyone cleans their plate at table. If there was too much food, or the glasses were over-filled, you wouldn't touch it."

Friday, May 6. Our idea of the height of luxury is watching a fisherman deliver three 12-pound King salmon to Bistro Ralph on the plaza in Healdsburg, which happened while Forrest and I were sitting at the counter for lunch. These were the first of the season, practically still dripping, just hours out of the water. The only way to the kitchen was right through the restaurant, and the fisherman was holding the salmon with his fingers under the gills. I thought the whole restaurant was going to stand up and applaud. There was no doubt what was going to be on the menu for dinner. The chef told us how he would prepare the salmon: simply grilled with organic leeks and a red wine sauce. He planned to drink the same wine he used in the sauce.

Simple Pinot Noir Sauce

Ingredients:
4 shallots, finely diced
¼ cup sweet butter
2 cups Pinot Noir
salt and pepper to taste

Directions:
Sauté the shallots in one tablespoon of butter over medium heat until soft but not brown. Add the wine. Bring to a simmer and reduce by a third. Add the remainder of the butter, whisking in a little at a time. Season with salt and pepper.

Pinot Noir with salmon is the fashion today, though the traditional choice would be Chardonnay. Forrest and I went to a winemaker dinner in Elk Grove, south of Sacramento, where the chef made scaloppine of salmon—thinly sliced and quickly pan-fried in a light beurre blanc sauce—which was perfect with Chardonnay. It struck me that we get so wrapped up in what's stylish that we tend to forget about the classics. David Berkeley, a Sacramento wine merchant and unofficial wine adviser to the White House, recommends adding a little sorrel to the butter sauce if you're serving Chardonnay.

An unusual but equally viable choice would be to serve a bottle of Pinot Gris with salmon. This is what Oregon winemaker David Lett suggests.

Sunday, May 8. Mother's Day. There's a whole new series of wildflowers around our house—blue bachelor's buttons, yellow lupine, and nodding Iceland poppies in red and pink that look like they're made of crepe paper. There must be seventy-five foxgloves growing around the Big House, each one individually staked, some over five feet tall. Just one in a tall vase in our living room is spectacular. Along with delphinium and columbine, foxgloves are very old-fashioned flowers. They last a long time because they shed their petals from the bottom up, not all at once.

Friday, May 13. Laughing at superstition, Forrest and I decided to have a Friday the Thirteenth party at our house. Brad Rubin, whose family distributes our wine in Massachusetts, was visiting, so we thought it would be nice to have everybody from the winery for an outdoor barbecue on our deck.

The party grew from there. We invited Jeff Dawson and his bride-to-be, Sharon; Tom Klaber, the editor of *Sonoma Style;* our friends Judge Matt Byrne and gallery owner Sandi Schlumberger.

There were about twenty of us that evening. We

served grilled lamb and mushroom kebabs, Ahi tuna brochettes, and Thai chicken satés. We had an old wine barrel, cut in half, filled with Brut, Fumé, and beer on ice. We always have beer on hand for winemakers at our house because sometimes after tasting wines all day, what you want is a cold beer. There's a saying in the wine business that it takes a lot of beer to make good wine. We had Zinfandel on the sideboard for red wine drinkers.

Our deck juts out from the back of our house. It faces one of our favorite blocks of Chardonnay, with wildflowers in the foreground. You can look up to the left and see the winery. Straight ahead is what we call the Meadow Warehouse, where we have 80,000 cases of sparkling wine aging *en tirage*—about three and a half years of inventory aging on the lees. Forrest and I wake up every morning, look out that way, and salute the future.

We have three trees growing out of our deck. The first, an old sycamore, was there when we bought the house. Forrest has trained it to be a big umbrella shading a queen-size wrought-iron bed and a wood table around which we can pull up as many as nine chairs. We planted the maple. Forrest bought it for me for my birthday. The white birch was a gift from my parents for our fourth anniversary.

We were all standing around on the deck, laughing and chatting, and Lisa Porter from our office was just about to tell me something about hearing loud, creaking noises when the whole deck collapsed. It pulled away from the house and crashed about four or five feet to ground level. Everyone screamed, and my niece Justine was crying. Plates and glasses slid to the ground. It was like being on a sinking ship. The grill tipped over, strewing burning coals. The deck had broken the water main as it fell, so Mark took the big jug of Alhambra water from the kitchen and dumped it all over the deck to douse the coals.

Fortunately, no one was hurt, and the party just moved inside. It was time for dessert, coffee, more sparkling, and brandy, all of which had been set up in the living room long beforehand.

"You sure know how to throw a party," said one guest as she was hoisted off the sunken deck and up into our kitchen. "Yeah, we bring the house down," said Forrest, but it will teach us—no more parties on Friday the Thirteenth.

Monday, May 16. My dad believes it is possible to have a perfect spring garden all at one moment. At Iron Horse, that moment occurs if the roses, azaleas, rhododendrons, and white wisteria bloom in unison. It happens about every five years.

The heart of his garden consists of about 200 roses, some the size of hats. Most are old roses, a gift to my parents when they acquired Iron Horse. A friend had purchased the Beverly Hills estate of Merle Oberon, but felt the antique English and French roses the actress had assembled were inappropriate for southern California. She therefore shipped them, bare-root, to

Iron Horse. Many of the labels were lost. Nevertheless, with some additions, an attempt was made—with rather successful results—to plant the stronger-colored roses at the bottom of the garden, gradually working up to the softer hues—silver-blues and soft lavender, including, of course, the Sterling rose, corals, pale pinks, creams, and last, white roses.

That is the formal rose garden. There are also pillar roses—some 9 feet tall—in beds near the Big House, a quarter mile of big cabbage-style Peace roses and white Kennedy roses running along the fence as you enter the property, climbing Cécile Brunners covering the potting shed, Mint Juleps grown as standards in old wine barrels in the 1920s corral where Forrest and I were married, deep, blood-red roses on the corral fences, and my favorite, an antique peach-colored rose that spirals 40 feet high in the large pine in front of our house. When it comes to roses, as with most things he's passionate about, Daddy has us on our knees while he's just hitting his stride.

My father and mother created their first garden when he was a young attorney in Los Angeles. It was pure white and very formal. At the time, he was heavily influenced by French gardens like those at Fontaine-bleau and Malmaison, Empress Josephine's home. In the south of France, he created a *jardin rouge*, all red flowers. In London, he had a 10-foot by 20-foot formal English walled garden. Iron Horse is very different from all these. His inspiration was Giverney, Monet's garden in Normandy. He says he was bowled over by the full palette of color there and that it opened his eyes to a more relaxed and free-form style of gardening, mixing colors and flowers from the heart instead of the head.

He is moving away from the concept that roses should stand alone. The German bearded iris bordering the roses was his first step in the direction of mixing other flowers and colors. This year he has jotted down that he wants to add anemones and freesias. Every so often, an errant red rose catches the eye amid the pastel-colored ones. "That would have driven me crazy twenty-five years ago," he says, smiling.

The main rose garden is divided into five sections by gravel pathways. In the center are a pair of white wisteria, cascading in front of a small arbor covered with white Honorine de Brabant. There's a Gothic-style wrought-iron chair perfectly placed for garden meditation. Father sometimes sits here.

The rhododendrons are planted in gradations of color. On the lower level, closest to the house and terraces, are the paler and earlier-blooming rhododendrons, including the almost white Gomer Waters. Walking higher on gravel paths and stone steps are rich pink Mrs. Whitneys, purples, and eventually deep reds, principally Radium, at the very upper part where the trees are more dense. The colors rise up the hill from light to dark. The lower colors are more tied to the house, in full view from the windows and verandas, and the stronger colors stand out against the darkness of the heavier foliage of the trees on the upper rim.

One of our favorite places for lunch is the stone terrace, where we can look down at the roses and up the hill to the azaleas, rhododendrons, calla lilies, foxgloves, and purple and white lunaria, called the money plant because after flowering its seed pods look like coins. There's columbine along the edge of the house and thick along the pathways and stairs up the hill. The woodland feeling is enhanced by clumps of wood hyacinth and forget-me-nots. Scattered among the rhododendrons are primroses still in bloom; they never actually quit, except in the middle of summer when it's too warm for them.

This is the setting where we entertained eighteen professional chefs who call themselves the Toques Blanches after the traditional white hats chefs wore (and often still wear) in the kitchen. Their organization is purely for the pleasure of socializing, eating, and drinking. We served polenta cooked in fig leaves with braised leeks, tomatoes, and artichokes with our 1993 Fumé Blanc; Sonoma baby lamb with salsa verde and 1992 Pinot Noir; and cherry galettes for dessert.

We roasted a whole lamb, weighing 14 pounds. To season the meat, pound the zest of two lemons, four cloves of garlic, one tablespoon of kosher salt, and one tablespoon of cracked black pepper in a mortar, then slowly add a quarter cup of olive oil to make a smooth paste. The lamb is rubbed with this mixture both inside the cavity and out, and is put in a 450 degree oven on a shallow roasting pan for fifty minutes. The tray is turned a few times for even browning. Test for doneness by inserting a meat thermometer into the haunch.

When the temperature reads 138 degrees, take the lamb out of the oven and allow it to rest for fifteen minutes, then place it on a large cutting board and chop into equal portions with a very sharp, heavy cleaver. Our chef Mark plates each dish with a small piece of leg meat, a piece of the loin, and a serving of the shoulder, drizzled with salsa verde. He adds a healthy portion of asparagus in May, French beans in July, and sautéd chard in August.

Everyone's salsa verde is slightly different. It's basically a combination of chopped fresh herbs—Italian parsley, oregano, thyme, and garlic. Forrest adds capers, anchovies, white wine vinegar, and olive oil to his. Some people use green olives in place of the capers, or lemon juice instead of vinegar. The secret is using fresh herbs.

We usually buy lamb from Bellwether Farms, where we also get delicious sheep's milk cheeses, and every summer we buy a prize-winning lamb at the Sonoma County Fair. It gets delivered to the back door of my parents' kitchen as a whole carcass.

My mother was a judge at the Sonoma-Marin fair for several years. One of the requirements for winning in the Future Farmer's division is that the youngsters cannot display emotion about selling their sheep. Any sentimentality leads to points off. "That's part of what they learn," she was told. "The sheep are not pets; they're bred to be sold."

Sonoma is famous for lamb. You see it on restaurant menus across the country. The flavor of the meat, like everything else, is determined by the environment, in this case our sweet green grass, hilly terrain, and cool climate.

Sonoma lambs were originally raised for wool. My mother's uncle was the largest wool merchant in the county. He had his own railway spur to make shipments to the east. The industry collapsed when big companies like Pendleton started buying from Europe, and the sheep ranchers had to change their direction. Now, in a classic example of what's old becoming new again, Forrest is thinking of raising sheep at T-bar-T to use as natural mowers in the vineyard.

Pinot Noir goes beautifully with spring lamb. The texture of the meat is softer and more delicate than beef and Pinot Noir is a soft, silky wine with rich fruit, a unique rose petal quality, and smoky undertones.

I have asked a number of chefs and wine experts why, how, or when they would choose a red Burgundy over a California Pinot Noir or one from Oregon. The answers have boiled down to why choose at all—just line them all up. There isn't one paintbrush that defines all California Pinot Noirs, any more than you can put all Burgundies in one category.

The style you choose would depend on what you're eating. We would pick a delicate Volnay for seared tuna and a Grands-Échezeaux for wild boar because it is richer and more structured, with a black-fruit, gamy flavor. California and Oregon wineries only increase the number of choices and broaden the spectrum from bright and soft to earthy and firm.

It takes a combination of soil and the winemaker's style to set one wine apart from another, but the quality and universality of winemaking today is such that the wines from all these regions have the potential to be on a par from the standpoint of quality. It's the same with Bordeaux versus California Cabernet Sauvignon. You could say it about any grape in every wine-producing area. The difference with Pinot Noir is that it is the hardest grape to grow, the most difficult wine to make, and the most frustrating to sell.

Pinot Noirs the world over are uneven vintage to vintage. In Oregon, many of the summers are too hot and humid for the grape. Burgundy's weather is also extremely difficult. It rains more often than not during harvest. As my mother says, "When they're good, they're very good, but when they're bad, they're terrible."

Burgundy is a labyrinth. There are 200 appellations contrôllée, and classifications within each of those. The caliber or renown of the shipper can be a reassurance, but the key is the grower and his vineyards. In just one appellation, there are 2,300 growers in the Côte d'Or alone, each with an average land holding of 5 hectares, often spread around several villages. This is because of the way the land was broken up after the French Revolution and because the laws of succession in France allow all children to inherit, not just the eldest. It is hard to imagine how they can make a living with such small parcels. The land value is unbelievable. Madame Lalou Bize, part owner of Domaine de la Romanée-

Conti and one of the most colorful personalities of Burgundy, bought 12 hectares in Vosne-Romanée in 1988 for 65 million francs—about $500,000 an acre, which is a very different league of farming.

California wine is more staightforward, but again you need to look at the winery and where the grapes were grown. Pinot Noir is very site-specific, unlike Chardonnay, which can be grown successfully in many different soils and climates, although even then each area imparts its own special characteristics. Pinot Noir does best in a cool, foggy, sheltered environment. The areas winemakers have identified as particularly suited for Pinot Noir include Santa Barbara; the Pinnacles, where Chalone is located; San Benito County; Carneros, which straddles Napa and Sonoma; Sonoma's Russian River area and Green Valley; Anderson Valley in Mendocino County; and Willamette Valley in Oregon.

I feel that it is thanks to Oregon that we've made such strides with Pinot Noir. Oregon was first to break the psychological barrier that Burgundy was automatically superior. This pushed those seekers of the holy grail in California to keep trying. It has only been in the last fifteen years that we've even learned where to grow Pinot Noir.

Pinot Noir is my mother's favorite wine. "It's my baby," she says, and personality-wise, it suits her to a tee—elegant, complex, and completely unpredictable. You never know what you're going to get out of the vineyard, out of the bottle, even out of one glass. Every sip can be different. It is sometimes refined, sometimes extravagant, sometimes surprisingly down-to-earth.

It also fits the foods we eat—little butter or cream and so many vegetables. The fruit and the acidity match the brightness and liveliness of the foods we enjoy. Pinot Noir also has the ability to carry meat as well as fish. It's a lighter red wine and though it's not sparkling, I love the way light shines through Pinot Noir. It casts a ruby sphere on your hand when you are holding the glass or on the tablecloth if you angle the glass in a certain way, a sight enchanting to contemplate while conversation continues around you.

Temperature is very important in serving Pinot Noir. It volatizes if it gets too warm—the acidity sticks out. It is better to slightly chill the wine by sticking the bottle in a bucket with ice and water or in the refrigerator for a few minutes.

If Pinot Noir seems too complex, there is a reward for becoming knowledgeable—a price break—because even a top Pinot Noir is often less expensive than a great Cabernet. The priciest California Pinot Noirs are from Williams Selyum at 75 dollars a bottle, or some of Callera's single-vineyard bottlings at 50 dollars retail, compared to the most sought-after Cabernets today, Caymus Special Selection, which sells for 100 dollars, when you can find it.

A similar buying strategy applies to other varietals as well. You can get a first-rate Sauvignon Blanc or Fumé Blanc with the same amount of money that would fetch just a middle-of-the-road Chardonnay. The main reason is the price of the grapes. A ton of ultra-premium Sauvignon Blanc in 1994 sold on the Napa grape market for $700 a ton compared to $1,600 a ton for the highest-quality Chardonnay.

I still wonder why the best red Burgundies are more expensive than comparable American Pinot Noirs. My interest is not in bringing them down but in helping us achieve those higher prices; it materially affects our lifestyle. So far, the only explanation that makes sense to me is that the difference is primarily perception, which, as one veteran of the wine trade told me, "Ain't nothing that three hundred years won't fix on its own."

May 27. The summer garden is being planted. It is quite a sight. José Puga, the head gardener, was shaking his head, "Your father wants many vegetables this year. Many vegetables." Actually, my father is the head gardener and José his lieutenant.

It takes four to five weeks to get all of the plants in the ground. First the ground is mowed, then disked. The furrows are dug. Lengths of black drip irrigation hoses are laid down. Two-foot-long wood stakes are angled into the dirt to hold up netting. There are two sections of tepee-style supports set up for pole beans beside the bush beans and three plantings of corn. The configuration changes every year to rotate the crops. At the end of each row are neat little white markers for each vegetable, naming all the varieties.

If my mother represents *abbondanza*, my father exemplifies utter abandon. He has 102 types of tomatoes this year, out of the 3,000 grown in California. The names alone are worth recording: Abe Lincoln, which is bright red; two that I feel should always be planted together — Big Boy and Ultra Girl; Evergreen, the yellow-green tomato of *Fried Green Tomatoes;* French varieties such as Marmande, Saint Pierre, and Merveilles du Marche; Brandywine, which is an Amish heirloom known since 1855 and used for canning and sauces; heart-shaped, meaty sauce tomatoes called Oxhearts; bicolored beef-steaks like Georgia Streak and Marvel Stripe; pretty pinks, purples, cherries, pear; yellow Russian, which looks like a persimmon; deep orange varieties like Nebraska Wedding; Black Krim, which is dark, deep red, almost black, sweet and tasty; Great White, a magnificent, almost perfect, large "white" tomato with low acidity, and Sweetie cherry tomatoes, which we eat like candy. There's one called Sausage tomato that is long and thin like a pepper and another type of cherry tomato that look like a sprig of currants.

They are all started from seed in mid-April, placed in small trays of potting soil, and kept in the hothouse until we are past the frost season — six vines each, anticipating the normal loss to gophers.

We have two major sections for tomatoes, one near the entrance adjacent to the creek, which tend to ripen very late, and a second area in the direct sun in the Lake Garden near the reservoir. Father has each variety planted in both locations to get the longest total growing season. They start bearing at the end of August and we are still harvesting at Thanksgiving.

Each vine is surrounded by a 4-foot-high wire cylinder to hold it up, theoretically to make picking easier, although often the most compelling, perfectly ripe tomatoes are out of reach, in the middle of the cage. Only my nieces, Justine and Barrie, can get their hands through the holes in the wires.

Father acquires his seeds from a dozen different catalog companies and seed-saver groups, organizations dedicated to preserving old-fashioned heirloom varieties by propagating and trading the seeds. He propagates his own seeds for only one type of tomato, a special French variety he likes, which is not otherwise available.

As if the tomatoes weren't enough, he has a dozen varieties of eggplant. They do best in the Lake Garden because it's warmer, and they range from glossy, midnight-purple globes to long and narrow Oriental varieties.

Between these two extremes lies a multitude of variations in size and form, including egg-sized Italians and finger-sized Orientals. There are white eggplants, rosy lavenders, which change color daily as they mature, and variegated varieties in all conceivable shapes and sizes. There's not much difference in taste, but color and texture can affect a dish. The globe eggplants are perfect for Asian dishes like shredded eggplant with dried shrimp. The Japanese and Chinese varieties are better for grilling and frying.

When it comes to hot peppers, there is no question that we grow too many. Father finds them irresistible.

His basic minimum requirement is to have all of the hot peppers represented on Mark Miller's Great Chili Poster. When the growing season is over we dry the hot chilies and hang them in swags from the rafters of the barn where we park the tractors.

Father's favorites are jalapeños for their distinct flavor and cayenne because they are small, easy to dry, and hot without being totally overwhelming. The hottest of the hot is the habañero—green, yellow, or orange and lantern-shaped like a small bell pepper. On the Scoville scale—devised by a Mr. Scoville using his tongue as the calibrating instrument to measure pungency—bells and pimientos are zero Scoville units, the serrano and Hungarian yellow between 7,000 and 25,000 units, and a mature habañero 300,000 units.

Mark Miller is the world's leading expert on chili flavors and certainly on chilies and wine. For fresh green chilies like New Mexico, Anaheim, jalapeño, and cayenne, which are grassy and earthy, he recommends Northern Italian whites, Viognier, white Rhône wines, especially blends like our Sauvignon Blanc-Viognier and Bonny Doon's Il Pescatore, which is Chardonnay, Pinot Meunier, Riesling, Roussanne, Pinot Blanc, and Pinot Noir, to balance their herbaceous complexity. For "tropical" chilies—habañero, Scotch Bonnet, Andean aji—he prefers Brut Rosé sparkling, Italian whites from Friuli because of their chestnut–acacia blossom nose, Alsatian Pinot Blanc, Riesling, Vin Gris and lighter reds like Beaujolais. For big, dried red chilies like anchos and mulatos, commonly used in molés, he also likes lighter reds—Mourvèdre from southern France, Syrah, Beaujolais, and Pinot Noir. These chilies have lots of tannin, which comes from the skins and the seeds—just like grapes—and again Mark says that blended wines, Rhône reds and classic Chiantis will have the advantage because they're multifaceted and offer several flavors beyond being simply refreshing.

The first sweet peppers in our garden to ripen are the yellows such as California bell and the prolific Gypsy, which later will turn orange and taste even sweeter. The red varieties include large crunchy Cadice and Italian style Corno di Toor or "bulls horn" peppers, which are delicious sautéed with fresh tomatoes, olive oil, garlic, and basil. Father's favorite is pepperoncini, a relatively small pepper, about 4 inches long and only an inch wide at the top, which ripens early and has the sweetest, richest flavor of all.

Most peppers turn from "green peppers" to their mature ripe color, which, depending on their breeding might be yellow, vivid, deep orange, or a chocolate that becomes rich brown in the middle of the season, then dark red at the very end. There is also a lilac bell which tastes like a crunchy green pepper but goes from a light lavender to a rich lilac color that holds over a long period of harvest, then gradually deepens to dark red.

The attraction of peppers is their variety. They have different colors, shapes, and flavors and they change while they're growing. We like to roast many different ones, primarily bells and Gypsy peppers, which have thicker skins and are easier to peel. Just lay them directly on the grill or over an open flame on top of the stove, turning them frequently until the skins are evenly blackened and charred all over but the flesh is still crisp. Then put them in a brown paper bag for ten minutes, which practically steams off the skins. We serve them peeled and sliced for crostinis on sliced, toasted baguette with a drizzle of olive oil and some young, fresh goat cheese. This is one of our favorite summer hors d'oeuvres with Fumé Blanc.

The most important precaution in growing peppers is keeping the sweet peppers separate from the chilies. This year Father received an odd order of seeds marked yellow bells, which he almost set aside until he noticed a sticker on the package that said: "This replaces your earlier shipment which was misidentified as yellow bells, but were in fact cayenne." Fortunately, he hadn't planted that "earlier shipment" yet, because it could have led to a very painful experience in the kitchen.

Summer squash seems benign but can be overwhelming. Father has zucchini in all its forms and colors— greens, yellows, variegated, long, round, short, Italian, French and Lebanese, his favorite, as well as sunny crooknecks, which my mother uses for table decorations, and five rows of round, scalloped squashes in white, pale green, dark green, and yellow. These were seeded by the end of the first week of May, then grown in flats in the glass house. There is a cornucopia of melons—pale yellow, orange, and deep red watermelons of all sizes, cantaloupes, casabas, muskmelon, and honeydews. The most exotic are the French Charentais and port melons, and even with them, though they look very much like American-style cantaloupes, there are a dozen varieties—mainly for staggered ripening times, but they have discernible flavor differences as well.

The Charentais melon is by far the most difficult to grow. The seedlings are planted on hills—four to a hill—at the end of May. They are highly susceptible to wire worm, a destructive larva, which has to be countered organically with nematodes, microscopic worms that seek out and eat soil-dwelling pests. Once past this problem, Charentais must be picked at their perfect moment of ripeness; you can't pick them green as they will ripen only on the vine, and you can't pick them too late as they have a tendency to overripen very quickly. On average, I would say one out of three that we pick is really at its peak moment when we cut it open in the kitchen, so there is tremendous loss, and Charentais have a shelf life of approximately seventy-two hours, which is why at Fouquet's on the Champs-Élysées you pay dearly for Charentais melon, which traditionally is served as an appetizer with prosciutto and a glass of champagne. If you want to stay on my dad's good side, it is best not to refer to such a luxury as mere cantaloupe.

May 27. There is a passage in the Song of Songs that perfectly describes this time of year in the vineyards. It's a romantic invitation: "Come, my beloved, let us go forth to the field; let us lodge in the villages. Let us get up early to the vineyards; let us see if the vine has budded, whether the grape blossoms are open, and the pomegranates are in bloom. There I will give you love."

Grape blossoms are the smallest flowers I have ever seen. They're little pinpoints of pale yellow. They have a very faint perfume, but it reaches a critical mass and fills the air when the whole vineyard is in bloom.

The flowering has just begun. We count on at least 110 days from now until harvest for sparkling and about 130 days for Cabernet at T-bar-T, the last grapes to be harvested. It could be shorter if the weather is too hot, or longer if the weather is too cold.

It's hard to get Forrest to relax in the vineyards. He's always pulling off leaves and checking their color. I'm convinced the vines talk to Forrest, telling him what they need, and while I wander along, Forrest feels pressured by all the work to be done. I've had a similar experience walking through the garden with my father, who sometimes sees only weeds and the flowers that need deadheading.

Forrest is frustrated. T-bar-T is looking too ragtag for his taste. Part of it is related to phylloxera. Every time he starts a project he has to break off to do the work needed on the vineyards being redeveloped, whether it's budding vineyard planted last year to Cabernet Sauvignon or putting up training wires for vineyard planted two years ago.

Budding—grafting a specific grape to disease-resistant rootstock—requires shoveling away the dirt around the rootstock so we can make the graft, cutting a notch in the bud, and securing the bud in place. We set a cardboard box around each vine—usually milk cartons with the bottoms cut out—to prevent sunburn and keep out the rabbits. Then we secure the carton with a shovelful of dirt around it.

Putting up training wires involves threading them by hand through the metal loops on the stakes all along each row. Both are highly labor-intensive and time-consuming. Meanwhile, the normal vineyard routine in May is green thinning and suckering—pulling off excess shoots along the fruiting part of the vine as well as at the trunk. This directs the energy of the vine, eliminates competition among too many shoots, and keeps the top of the vines open so sunlight will filter through to the flowers, from which the fruit will set in a few weeks. This too requires a lot of manpower.

Iron Horse seems much further along than T-bar-T because with no phylloxera there isn't the distraction of replanting. The vineyards here are all established and fit more into a routine. However, Forrest feels certain blocks even at Iron Horse are looking a little "ragged" because of their age. Block C has a bacterial infection commonly known as dead arm, usually found in older vineyards. It affects the circulatory system of the plant. The cure—other than just coping with it—is called body replacement, which means cutting the vine down to about a foot in height and letting it grow a new shoot, interrupting production for a year. The prime of a vine's life is twenty-five to thirty years—about the time for a new generation to take over in a winemaking family.

Walking through Block B, Forrest remarked that vines are like people—the early health of a vine affects its whole life. If it's stunted, lacking in nutrients, training, or water, it will grow strangely and can never be retrained to perfection. These old vines can make wonderful wine but are much more difficult to farm because there's no uniformity. It's as if there are 10,000 individuals out there, as compared to Block O, planted in 1984, which looks like a regiment of perfect little soldiers. The new sections also produce individual wines depending upon soil shifts, slope, sun exposure, and all the rest; they just aren't so idiosyncratic to farm.

We wound our way home via the Lake Garden. For dinner, Forrest made roast chicken with steamed rice flavored with the roasting juices and fresh garden peas—our first of the year—stir-fried with onions and shiitake mushrooms. We had Brut in the refrigerator, which we sipped while Forrest was cooking, and he poured about a cup's worth into the pot that he used to steam the peas before adding them to the wok. The rest we drank with dinner.

Monday, May 31. Memorial Day weekend. The Memorial Weekend Parade and Livestock Auction in Healdsburg marks the unofficial start of summer. It's still a farm town parade, featuring truckloads of kids, primarily from organizations like Future Farmers of America and 4-H, which stands for head, heart, hand, and health. Some of the oldtimers ride along in antique cars or mounted on Arabian show horses and Peruvian Pasos with silver-studded saddles.

Forrest started spending his boyhood summers in Sonoma County in 1950 when his parents bought their ranch in the Alexander Valley. The valley was planted mostly in prune orchards then and didn't switch to grape growing until the late '60s. Forrest witnessed the influx of wealthy winery owners, San Franciscans with second homes and tourists who flocked to Healdsburg in the summer. His parents were in the vanguard.

Forrest remembers the family driving up to the ranch every Friday night in the summertime with groceries and stopping at Pedroncelli to stock up on Pedroncelli's dry Rosé.

For parties at T-bar-T, Forrest's mother would serve a huge New York strip that was done charred and rare the way she learned to cook it from Pierre Bercut of Bercut Bros., the most famous butchers in San Francisco in the '50s, located on Market Street near Powell. First she rubbed cracked pepper and prepared mustard over the meat, put it under the broiler for fifteen minutes on each side to seal in the juices, then lowered the oven temperature to 450 degrees and cooked it for thirty-five to fifty minutes. She sliced it thin and served it with her special peach chutney. Vic Bergeron, the founder of Trader Vic's, was always after her to sell him the chutney recipe, but she refused, mainly because in truth there was no recipe. She made it differently each time. Forrest says her secret was using underripe peaches, lots of coriander and lime, and cooking it down very slowly for a long time. He says she would start out with ten quarts and end up with four pints of very concentrated, tangy chutney that was sweet, tart, and spicy, all in one mouthful.

These days, Healdsburg is caught between two exits off Highway 101, but it still looks like a Mark Twain kind of town. The local kids go swimming in the Russian River, and vineyard workers wearing blue jeans, boots, and summer cowboy hats of straw fill the park benches in the plaza in the late afternoon.

Everything centers on the elegant town square, where the old buildings have been turned into restaurants, bakeries, three or four coffee houses with more to come, a great men's clothing store, wine-tasting bars, galleries, and home furnishing shops. Eventually you run into everyone there. You don't go to Downtown Bakery unless you expect to be seen.

Healdsburg is a very, very small town. You can shoot a cannon down any street after eight o'clock at night. As recently as 1981, the opening of a Long's drugstore was front-page news for three days. In 1991, the opening of a McDonald's was cause for protest. There used to be a lot of bikers who'd hang out around the plaza, at bars like John and Zeek's, but all the pool halls are gone now.

The downside of gentrification is that the shoe repair man who took care of everyone's shoes in town has gone out of business. Healdsburg runs the risk of becoming one of those terribly sweet towns like Carmel and St. Helena where you just cannot imagine living. But if you go one block off the plaza, you'll still find the old barbershop, insurance offices, and a growing number of Hispanic businesses. It's the mix, the diversity, that will be Healdsburg's saving grace.

June

Feast Days: Summer Solstice, Our Anniversary

Thursday, June 3. I'll tell you when Iron Horse is at its best—evening at 8, sundown. Today there was a light breeze off the ocean refreshing the vineyard. The whole place was bathed in a golden light that made the top of the vine leaves look yellow. You can almost see the leaves drinking in the sunlight through their tips. The air is moist, there's a smell of lavender, jasmine, and wild blackberries, and the whole vineyard in bloom.

Our house is sweet with daylilies, my second favorite flower after roses. They vary in color from pure yellow to pale salmon pink, with the occasional ruddy pink, lining the road to the winery under the palms and olives, covering a hill near one of the barrel rooms and filling another hill in front of Laurence and Terry's house. They are in terra-cotta pots all around the Big House and in a secret spot, hidden by redwoods and other evergreens, where nobody goes except for seclusion—and in June to see the daylilies.

Mixed among the palms on the way to the Big House are pomegranates with bright red blossoms that last through July, ornamental loquats, which bloom in May, with leaves that turn red for summer, and fuzzy, silvery pink smoke bushes. Along this same drive are yucca, red-hot pokers, and tall, slender, white and magenta Watsonia lilies.

Fuchsias as fat as the hummingbirds they attract have been brought out of the hothouse and placed along the stone garden wall in front of the dining room alcove. In the beds behind the fuchsias wild impatiens grow like weeds with miniature orchidlike mauve and white flowers. Father pulls them out later in the summer when they get too bushy, after they've reseeded themselves, replacing them with traditional white impatiens. There used to be a fountain of jasmine hanging from an old Monterey cyprus that shades the round table where we normally have lunch in the summertime. I worried that it was moving too far away from its roots, seeking more sunlight, which put it at risk. It was turning brown and eventually stopped blooming. Now it has been pulled out, though Father promises to replace it because I miss it.

The hydrangea are beginning to bloom. Some are mixed among the ferns where the water trickles down from the grotto and others are scattered on the hill. Although they were originally hand-picked from various sources to be pure white, our soil caused some to revert to their original heritage of pinks and blues. They bloom all summer and in the autumn we pick them as everlastings that dry beautifully.

There's also a smattering of roses now. Rich, deep blue delphinium stand out as the best of show while the cutting garden is in transition. Gladiolas, alternating beds of white and pink cosmos, and traditional zinnias are being planted to bloom later in the summer in pink, white, and Mother's favorite, Green Envy.

Wild sweet peas are scattered out in the fields near our house in the unplanted areas by the creek. There are more pomegranates in bloom down here, and halfway in between, at the crossroads to the winery, stand hedges of exotic guava blossoms and bottlebrush, long and bristlelike, colored an unusual shocking pink instead of the typical red.

We've been gorging ourselves on cherries. We've never had a crop this big. We usually get so few that they are doled out like jewels. This year we have four full trees. Forrest and I have been bringing home whole bagsful at peak ripeness every night for a week. We've been eating them with Brut Rosé at sunset and after dinner for dessert. We've served them to guests at every lunch and Mark has been cooking with them. I have probably eaten an entire tree's worth myself. I'm afraid I may turn into a cherry.

We are also competing with the birds for loquats. Almost every day we are able to get one to two flats of raspberries. Strawberries, boysenberries, and ollallie berries are close to ripe.

The vegetable garden is producing enough lettuce to feed an army. We have sweet carrots, peas, spring bunching onions, and small fingerling potatoes. We are finally at the end of the fava beans, and the artichokes are starting to turn to flower.

Friday, June 10. Today was the start of the fire season. Who says we don't have seasons in California; we have earthquakes, drought, fire, and mudslides. It was 105 degrees at T-bar-T, 100 at Iron Horse, 95 in San Francisco. They don't know what to do in the city. San Francisco is simply not equipped for such weather. Usually we expect fog in June.

Fire weather is when it's hot and dry. Even a faint breeze feels breathless and offers no refreshment. Worse yet is a hot, heavy wind that seems capable of spontaneous combustion.

Forrest had a 75-acre fire at T-bar-T this year. It was sparked by two windblown utility lines that touched. The flames ran up the hill behind the foreman's house into the tall trees—too steep for the Department of Forestry to get any equipment up to it. They had to fight the fire on foot with shovels. Forrest's son, Michael, was on one of the fire lines. He says he could feel the heat come through his shoes. The next day, the fire lines looked like hundreds of feet of marked hiking trails. I imagine Michael will always remember the night he and the foreman, Victor Arreola, helped save the ranch.

Monday, June 19. Forrest is shocked that it's nine months since the last harvest. He will start blending Chardonnay next week. All the various lots are coming out of barrel after nine months aging on the lees, the spent yeast cells, what the French call *"sur lie."*

To set the stage for assembling the blend, we organize a style tasting to evaluate our wines against the competition. Hypothetically, we could fall in love with another Chardonnay, which might inspire us to move in a new direction or see a nuance of our style that we hadn't seen before, which may lead us to accentuate that particular quality or, conversely, to put on a little makeup.

We tasted twenty-six wines from California, Burgundy, Australia, and New Zealand, including two of our own, in two flights, that is, in two sessions, fourteen wines at a time. We tasted all of the wines blind. Andy, who did not participate in the tasting, opened all the bottles, mixed up the order, and put them in numbered brown paper bags. There's a natural tendency to search for our own wines in a blind tasting, which kind of defeats the purpose, though it's not a foregone conclusion that we will like our wines best.

The most unmistakable lesson from such a tasting is that not everyone likes the same wines. Number 4 stood out as one I couldn't even bring to my lips. The smell of malolactic was so heavy I rejected it on nose alone. It turned out to be a 1993 Sonoma Chardonnay that *The Wine Spectator* gave a 92 rating. Shows you what I know.

Overall, we perceived three basic schools of Chardonnay—clean and crisp, full-blown, and sweet, though within each one is a spread of styles.

Iron Hose falls in the clean, crisp category, which to me means bright fruit, the opposite of earthy. It also means technically flawless. The crispness comes from naturally lively acidity and a cool climate. Acidity comes across as lemony and juicy—mouth-watering.

The full-blown style is what California Chardonnay is famous for—a big, buttery quality usually created by very ripe fruit, which attests to a warmer climate, malolactic fermentation, and extended time on the lees. Malolactic fermentation is practically ubiquitous in California Chardonnays. Three I can think of that do not have malolactic are Iron Horse, Far Niente in Napa, and one of Sanford's bottlings in Santa Barbara.

Sweet simply means there is residual sugar—most commonly achieved by adding unfermented grape juice, what the French call *"mute,"* to whatever percentage you want. Recently a Texas woman asked me which is drier—Chardonnay or French Chablis, which just five years ago would have been laughable as both are made from the Chardonnay grape and equally dry, but today it depends on which California Chardonnay because so many now are made to be sweet.

The second flight was another set of fourteen Chardonnays, which had scored 89 or higher in *The Wine Spectator*. The two repeats were ours, though this time I reversed my order of preference. I liked our master blend over Cuvée Joy, confirming that after tasting a certain number of wines, the more delicate styles tend to get lost in the shuffle. We also remarked on how much diversity there had been in the first flight, and how homogeneous they seemed in the second. It may have been that our taste buds were tired, making it more difficult to discern nuances.

Two weeks later, we staged another tasting of lower Russian River Chardonnays—eight wines from within a five-mile radius, including Green Valley. There's a distinct Russian River flavor—a citrusy, spicy quality specific to the area—though each of these wines expressed it a little differently. Here are my tasting notes:

#1. Very smooth, delicate, sweet fruit (not sugar), not one drop of oak. Very appealing. This wine retails for $9.99 a bottle.

#2. Very good. Earthy (could be French were it not for the bright fruit). "Leesy" or yeasty which gives it a certain fullness, but still crisp and clean. Elegant.

#3. Can smell some weight on the nose (partial malolactic?), but finishes clean and refreshing. I get burnt lemon zest in the finish. This was my third favorite.

#4. Perfectly clean. Lighter in weight. Most complex fruit. My favorite.

#5. Not as complex. At a disadvantage compared to the wine before. A tad short in the finish. This turned out to be the most expensive wine in the flight.

#6. Malolactic and sweet.

#7. More malolactic and very yeasty, a highly distinctive style, unmistakably Dehlinger, our closest neighbor, just one mile to the east of us. It's a full temperature degree warmer at Dehlinger than here.

#8. Sweet. Burnt matchstick in the finish. Very much a winemaker's wine. More technique-driven than fruit. Gets excellent ratings.

June 20. These are our salad days. We have a full selection. My father spends the winter hunting for seeds and now is when we reap the benefit.

No other lettuce tastes quite like my dad's lettuce. First of all, it's the freshness. And he has so many different types. But I am convinced there is a distinct flavor to our greens, that *goût de terroir* applies to vegetables as much as it does to grapes. I'm told that it holds for flowers as well—Bulgarian roses, for example, are more intense and more highly prized for perfume than any other. I've heard of an almond grower who can distinguish the taste of the almonds in one section of his orchard from another. Likewise with oysters—the same species of oyster will taste different from different waters. Far from being mysterious, it seems that *goût de terroir* is simply a law of nature.

Father is always seeking out new field greens from catalogs and seed markets everywhere he travels. They are all started in flats in the greenhouse, thinned and planted out in May, with successive new plantings every two weeks so we are never without. Favorites include red and green romaines, crispy batavias with red-tipped leaves, big rosettes of Bibb or limestone, oakleaf and red oakleaf selected for their unusual shape as well as their delicate, sweet flavor, and deertongue lettuce, also called rodin, which has a very pretty lime-green color, sometimes blush tipped, a special buttery flavor, and a unique crispy texture. For years, Father refused to plant plain old iceberg because it was the only lettuce his mother ever served, but iceberg happens to be one of my mother's favorites, so this year he relented and when they dine alone, that's frequently what he gets, with blue cheese dressing and a crisp, bright Sauvignon Blanc or a Sancerre.

We love wine and salad. The combination is supposed to be an oxymoron. However, there would be an uprising in California if we couldn't have wine with our salads.

Salad depends on its positioning in the meal and the choice of greens. We love an appetizer course of baked goat cheese on a bed of bitter greens, which is delicious with Fumé Blanc.

We frequently use crisp, firm greens like chicories for warm duck, lamb, or beef salad, which changes the wine choice to Pinot Noir and also lessens the need for much more than olive oil for a dressing mixed with the pan drippings. If served after the main course, we might choose spicy arugula with a strong cheese and a young vintage of our Cabernets.

I, of course, drink sparkling wine with many salads: a traditional Caesar, Chinese chicken salad, or an endive and beet salad served with a light, creamy horseradish vinaigrette. There is a special affinity between horseradish and champagne because they both have good acidity.

A small garden salad with a vinaigrette dressing is perhaps the hardest match with wine. The intense acidity of vinegar has the effect of reducing the taste of acid in any wine served with it. It makes wine taste flat or flabby. One recommendation is to counteract the vinegar or another high-acid ingredient in a dish with a white wine that is also assertive and high in acid, such as a Sancerre or its California alternative, Sauvignon Blanc.

Generally speaking, balsamic vinegar is less harsh on wine than other vinegars, though it still has to be used sparingly. Father prefers his own Chardonnay vinegar because it is even milder than balsamic. To show that it's not just personal bias, he feels his own Pinot Noir vinegar is too strong for salad.

Some days we don't like to interfere with the integrity of a particularly flavorful green so we use no dressing at all. More often than not, we toss a mixture of greens with a little olive oil, sometimes adding a splash of orange or lemon juice and salt.

Besides keeping the vinegar low, another way to mix

salad with various wines is by adding an accent that ties to the wine. Walnuts, apples, and pears are good with Chardonnay and Pinot Noir because they share the same flavors. Hazelnuts or fresh, sweet peppers are complementary to Cabernet Sauvignon—cabernets often have a distinctive bell pepper characteristic. Sliced avocado complements sparkling—the richness of avocado goes with the creaminess of sparkling.

As an insight into the lettuce business, today's price for organic salad mix in the supermarket is $8.99 a pound, compared to what it was in February, when lettuce from Sonoma is shipped by the container load back east. A case—24 heads, weighing about 24 pounds—costs 18 dollars wholesale in the wintertime. The price drops to its lowest in August when a grower is lucky to get 8 dollars a box.

Who knows what anything is worth? Artichoke flowers, which we have by the hundreds, sell for 75 cents apiece in the market. I was surprised to see garlic flowers for sale when we have such an abundance. I put together a massive bouquet of them with wild mint flowers for the kitchen. Blueberries are 24 dollars a flat. And if that doesn't beat all, driving down Highway 116, right before the freeway entrance, there's a big container, like a U-Haul or recycling bin, with a sign that reads: WANTED: USED JEANS. WILL PAY UP TO $16 FOR LEVI 501s.

Friday, June 24. Our anniversary. Forrest has been counting grape clusters all week. "Do you know what

I see when I close my eyes?" he asked. "I see clusters."
For our anniversary I went with him to T-bar-T, where
he had thirty acres to go. Up and down the rows, every
tenth vine, counting clusters. He wants to know how
much wine we will make this year. There are about
twenty-five clusters per vine, which, after the fruit is
harvested, pressed and fermented, will yield a bottle's
worth of wine. I lasted about two hours, then fell asleep
under a spreading oak. It was very warm, dry, and
dusty. The wild oats on the hills surrounding the vineyard were completely dried out and golden. It smelled
like summer at T-bar-T, with a faint aroma of grapes.
A breeze picked up the sweet smell of the dried oats,
which is particularly intense and lingering where they're
trampled down like straw. The chaff and dust in the
air make your nose itch. You can feel the heat rising
off the ground as the breeze from the ocean blows it
out of the low spots where it accumulates.

I picked wild thistles, dock, timothy grass, and some
of the oats for our living room. Forrest teases me that
I love the weeds. With all the flowers we have around
here, I'm out picking weeds. I keep telling him that one
person's weed is someone else's flower.

When we returned to Iron Horse, we were struck by
the coolness and the change in colors. The "home" vineyard is so lush. Everything is green—the riparian corri-
dor, the blackberries, the vines, the willows, the firs
and redwoods in the hills. The vines have grown as
much as a foot since flowering. They all look very even
and happy, gently rustling in the breeze with the fog

waiting in the wings to refresh the air at night. "We're making progress," said Forrest. "We ought to have the vineyard looking the way we want it by about two weeks before harvest."

At sunset we went into the garden to pick lettuce, several kinds of basil, and raspberries for our anniversary dinner. The basil smelled like perfume as we carried handfuls into the house. Forrest made salmon stuffed with lemon slices, fresh basil, salt, and pepper, which he wrapped in aluminum foil and baked in the oven for an hour at 375 degrees. He served it with a *sauce vert*—fresh basil, fresh parsley, extra virgin olive oil, salt, and pepper pureed in the Cuisinart, and then warmed to be spooned over the salmon. We had oven-roasted potatoes as a side dish and baby greens with a fresh raspberry vinaigrette—all of which tasted delicious with Brut Rosé, even the salad because there was so little vinegar and so many raspberries.

We had no trouble finishing the bottle of wine. There's a story that wine comes in a 750 ml. bottle because it's the perfect size for a couple to enjoy. The traditional formula is that a bottle holds five 5-ounce glasses of wine, which means two people would get two and a half glasses each. The first to break the ice. The second to make you amorous. And all that's left is another half glass each because a full third glass would be too much. It's all based on romance.

June 27. There are about thirty barrels sitting in front of the winery. They're empty. Each lot or group of

Chardonnay barrels is being transferred into stainless-steel tanks in preparation for blending. The barrels are then washed and stored in a dry cellar until harvest, when they will receive a new vintage.

We have about 700 barrels dedicated to Chardonnay: one-third new oak; one-third one year old; one-third two years old.

Tonight we're sulfuring in the vineyard to guard against mildew. We'll get plenty of calls in the morning. I'm sure we'll hear from the masseuse who lives down the road. The last time we sulfured she called to complain that the tractor made her massage table vibrate.

We spray sulfur by night when the wind calms down, which is usually around midnight.

July

Feast Days: Forrest's Birthday, Fourth of July, Bastille Day

July 2. My parents have invented a new drink: the Sterlini, which is Brut with fresh plum juice. We are not purists about adding fruit to wine. A handful of berries in a glass of sparkling or Sauvignon Blanc is delicious. Mother makes a Sonoma sangria with Sauvignon Blanc, peaches, and fresh sweet peppers. As with everything else our greatest extravagance is the ingredients, which means using the best wine and fresh, flavorful, ripe fruit.

July 4. I know I am spoiled. I realized it when I ordered a tuna sandwich the other day at the Jimtown Store in the Alexander Valley and was surprised it wasn't grilled fresh tuna on a baguette. Even Forrest thought I was kidding. Though he's in no position to talk. His idea of a perfect hamburger is as carefully prepared as foie gras and includes eating it with a glass of Zinfandel. I would just as soon drink sparkling with pizza as anything else—the yeastiness of the crust matches the yeastiness of sparkling, and I would also make a strong case for Brut Rosé with barbecue.

According to Joshua Wesson, a wine and food expert, this is not the way most Americans think. "Americans are historically ambivalent about wine," he says. "We deem it appropriate for Dover sole, but not for the food we eat every day, whereas it would be unthinkable for a Frenchman to enjoy a croque monsieur *sans* a glass of Beaujolais." A croque monsieur is essentially a ham and cheese sandwich and, in fact, sandwiches are very compatible with wine because of the bread. What could be more basic?

In matching wine with sandwiches, Josh recommends thinking about what goes with the condiments—crisp, dry Rieslings or champagne with mayonnaise, Chardonnay with mustard, Chenin Blanc or white Zinfandel (yes, white Zinfandel) with ketchup or Russian dressing, real Zinfandel—red Zinfandel—with barbecue.

You can also make certain, basic cultural connections like matching an Alsatian wine with hot dogs or with lamb sausage on toasted baguette with sauerkraut and whole-grain mustard. Or, the complete antithesis-Chinese-style barbecued spareribs, which are sweet and aromatic, with a refreshing, unoaked, fruity Chardonnay.

Summertime is supposed to be easy and fun, and that goes for what we eat and drink, too. It's just too hot for Cabernet Sauvignon. Lighter reds served slightly chilled have much more appeal in the same way that simple, cool cotton looks and feels better in summer than heavy velvet and brocade. The same logic applies to white wines. Full-blown, rich, opulent Chardonnays are difficult to swallow when it's 90 degrees and humid.

I remember driving from Paris to the south of France for summer vacation. This had to have been 1968. I was fourteen years old. One of our stops was Paul Bocuse's famous restaurant in Collonges-au-Mont-d'Or, just north of Lyons. Anticipating a three-star experience, Daddy had ordered our meal a month in advance — escargots, coq au vin, salad, and a selection of aged cheeses, followed by oeufs à la neige, an elaborate meringue dessert. He had even discussed the wines at great length on the phone with the chef, deciding on a bottle of Château Grillet up front and a Richebourg for the main course. But it turned out that our reservation at Bocuse was on the hottest day of the year, the worst traffic day of the year, compounded by our getting lost and the car boiling over. We had no appetite when we arrived at the restaurant. Paul Bocuse himself met us at the door, told us he had canceled our entire meal, and sat us down to a simple, relaxing, cold boeuf à la mode and a bottle of chilled, fresh Beaujolais. He said we didn't have to pay for it if we didn't like it, but that food and wine should match the mood and weather. We were relieved and the meal was perfect.

Some wines seem to span the seasons. Fumé Blanc goes from early spring to summer along with the vegetables and it will linger into fall at least until the end of tomato season, but rosés are quintessentially summer wines—light, refreshing, best when chilled. A good rosé is what M. F. K Fisher called "go down easy drinkin' stuff." Living in France, she knew rosés well "and how they can be plain and still subtle, and sturdier than dry whites, but never pretentious."

Rosés are part of my childhood. My brother and I grew up spending our summers in the south of France. We had a home in a village called Castelaras in the hills behind Cannes near Mougins. The whole village was designed by Jacques Quelle, an avant-garde architect. Our house was shaped to capture the best light at every time of day. There was one balcony where you could read by the light of the full moon. My room faced the sea. I remember how I felt waking up in the morning. My bedcovers were white with bright daisies. French doors opened onto a small half-moon-shaped balcony. The sky was so blue and open-ended. I felt very happy there. Life seemed carefree, and now, ordering a bottle of Domaines Ott, even in the dead of winter in a Chinese restaurant, brings back extremely sunny memories.

My brother says people take rosés too seriously, or we're suspicious because of the color that they're going to be sweet when in many ways a dry, simply made rosé may well be the more sophisticated choice exactly because of its nonchalance.

Freshness is the key to these wines. They don't age well. Nor do they travel well.

Rosés come in many shades. They are made from a variety of red-skinned grapes—Grenache grapes are used in the Rhône valley, Cabernet Franc dominates the Loire; rosés from Provence are made from Carignan, Grenache, and Cinsault. Vin Gris de Pinot Noir is the local drink of Burgundy; rosato de Sangiovese is indigenous to Tuscany. White Zinfandel is all ours.

White Zinfandel, known for its sweet, fruity flavor and pretty color, is made by separating the skins from the juice immediately after crushing and by stopping fermentation before all the sugar is converted into alcohol. The farmers are happy because they like being able to sell their grapes at 19 degrees Brix; they get their crop off the vine early, with less risk, and still get a good price. For wineries, it is a great cash flow product. You can bring in the grapes, crush, and in a month bottle and sell without worrying about two years of winemaking.

The problem with white Zin is that it's sweet and unsophisticated; but it has saved many old Zinfandel vineyards that otherwise would have been pulled out. And now, of course, the wines from these old vines are highly sought after to make red Zinfandel.

Other grape varieties commonly pressed for rosé include Cabernet Sauvignon, Syrah, and Tempranillo. Generally, the darker the grape, the better the rosé. Some cheap rosés are simply blends of red and white wines.

July 14. The lavender mixed with the daylilies makes walking down Palmolive Drive feel like Provence. Agapanthus, the exotic lily of the Nile, look so cool and crisp in a solid bank near the presses behind the main winery building. There's more of that Provence feeling in the vegetable garden by the creek because of all the squash blossoms.

There are zinnias of all colors in the cutting beds. My mom's way of arranging them is either a bouquet of one color or a series of vases, each with a different color. It's hard to find seed packets of single colors, particularly whites and greens. At our house, I tend to mix them all together.

My father has a fancy for green flowers—green calla lilies, which he grows from seed, green zinnias, mint julep roses, and pale green gladiola called Irish Linen— just starting to come out, finally, weeks after everyone else in the county has had them. This is one of the discreet indications of how much cooler we are in Green Valley in the summer, and just as the flowers are slowed down by weeks, so too are the grapes.

For wildflowers, aka weeds, there's yellow Scotch broom, yarrow, wild sweet peas, which add pink to other dried grasses, and everlastings like German statice and cattails, which we lacquer with hair spray so they won't explode all over the living room as they dry out. Queen Anne's lace comes out at the end of August or beginning of September, along with some thick spikes with very pretty yellow flowers and some tall lacy bushes with delicate pink blossoms that grow around the reservoir. I asked Forrest what they were. "Weeds," he told me. I asked Father the name of another plant with a tall stalk and yellow flowers growing on the bank on the way up to the winery, just before Manuel Briano's house, and his answer, too, was "Weeds."

July 21. Father says he is watching his first tomato. It's half yellow and half green. "I'm waiting for it with bated breath," he said. In the meantime, we can't eat enough zucchini to make a dent and by late July we can't even give it away. It's like science fiction: "The Zucchini That Ate Summer." I go picking in the garden with Father and he follows behind me saying, "Joy, you missed some," and I say, "No, Daddy, they just grew since the time I walked by."

Sometimes Mark prepares an all-vegetarian dinner in an effort to use up some of the bounty from the garden. Tonight we had French beans tempura with 1993 Fumé Blanc, stuffed "ronde de Nice" zucchini and 1978 Jaboulet "La Chapel" Hermitage from Father's cellar, followed by dried jack cheese and Gravenstein apple pie with 1989 Demi-Sec.

For the main course, Mark sliced four large squash in half crosswise, which he hollowed out with a spoon, leaving a half inch of flesh, which he seasoned with salt and pepper. (If you can't find rondes de Nice, patty pan or large zucchini work just as well.)

The stuffing is essentially a ratatouille made with two Japanese eggplants, peeled and diced; two sliced zucchini; two sliced crookneck squash; two julienned red peppers; two julienned red onions; four tomatoes, peeled, seeded, and cubed; one cup of pitted green olives; two tablespoons of capers, rinsed in water; two tablespoons of fresh Italian parsley; olive oil; kosher salt; and freshly ground pepper.

To make the stuffing, put the eggplants, zucchini, and squash in a bowl and toss with a teaspoon of salt. Sauté the onion and peppers in two tablespoons of olive oil over medium-high heat until caramelized and then remove and set aside. Sauté the crooknecked squash, zucchini, and eggplant in two more tablespoons of oil, until golden-brown.

Toss together the sautéd eggplant and squash, the caramelized red pepper and onion, the tomatoes, olives, capers, parsley, and ground pepper and spoon into the hollowed-out squash. Set in a roasting pan and allow to bake in a 350 degree oven for forty-five minutes.

This was a family dinner, which is rarer than you might think. We all live on the property and work for the winery, but usually we're zooming in eight different directions, or we have guests, so there never seems to be any time to talk. One of the ways we define ourselves as a family is by gathering for a meal.

My parents are the catalyst for family dinners. Mother calls everyone that morning and Daddy reiterates the invitation in the office. For us they put as much energy into how the table looks and how the food and wines are presented as for company. They do the same for themselves. My father will say, "Who better than us?" when he brings out a special vintage for family.

He has only one or two bottles of this particular vintage of Hermitage remaining in his cellar. The wine was bought on one of his December forays in Lyons, where he would visit his favorite wine merchants while Mommy shopped for quennelles, truffled sausages, and chocolates. Thomas Jefferson made similar trips heading south through France, following the same route at the same time of year, and he too would stop to see his favorite wine merchant with whom he corresponded over the years.

My parents would normally serve Hermitage with game or a selection of aged cheeses. It is a long-lived, deeply colored, peppery wine made for hearty food, and though this evening's dinner was vegetarian, it was still quite substantial and called for a sturdy accompaniment.

One of the attributes of an Hermitage is how it evolves in the glass over the hour or two we linger at the table. The wine is part of what keeps us in our seats long enough for everyone to relax.

My favorite family dinners are the ones that dissolve into tears of laughter. Then I think about the famous first sentence of *Anna Karenina* that all happy families are alike.

Were only the unhappy ones interesting? Today it seems the opposite is true: a happy family is much more dramatic.

July 28. There's a handwritten sign on the side of the road outside Forestville that reads: "Corn, Zucchini, Basil." We don't have corn yet, but clearly just one mile to the east, they do. Ours won't be ready for at least another month. Zucchini? They must be kidding. As for basil, we have six different kinds: Thai basil, which we use in curries and Asian-style salads, often served with Brut; lemon basil for roasting fish, which is delicious with Chardonnay; cinnamon basil with field greens, which tends to skew the salad toward Pinot Noir, and three Italian basils. With traditional Genoa basil and tomatoes, my father recommends a cool glass of rosé or a light, peppery, fruity Rhône wine. Mark likes grilled bread dipped in pesto with a glass of Fumé Blanc. With vegetable soup and pistou he prefers a Bandol like Domaine Templier. Forrest loves cold salmon and pesto with Pinot Gris or its Italian equivalent Pinot Grigio. He says the bright, fresh green flavors call out for equally bright, fresh, crisp whites. He prefers red wine—Sangiovese or Zinfandel—if the pesto sauce is on pasta.

Sunday, July 31.   Garden club tea. Father's ideas about gardening have definitely mellowed. One lone pink cosmos has somehow rooted itself with the sunflowers. He thought about pulling it out but decided to let it be. "It's actually very charming," he said.

This change in attitude—at least toward gardening—was reinforced by an article Nigel Nicolson wrote about his mother, Vita Sackville-West, and Sissinghurst, her garden in Kent. According to Nicolson, his mother deeply believed that gardening was a process—that a full-blown rose with decaying petals has its own kind of beauty and that a garden with no brown leaves is artificial. She also apparently felt that if there were no mistakes in your garden, you were playing it too safe.

It was in this frame of mind and on the day after bringing Mother home from the hospital following knee surgery that my father entertained eighty elderly members of the a west coast horticulture society, mainly blue-haired ladies, who arrived in a bus, for tea.

Mother had arranged for two tables covered with crisp, white linen tablecloths to be set up on the grass terrace. Tea was pitchers of home-grown mint ice tea, giant bowls of strawberries and raspberries, chocolate brownies, and sparkling wine, though we had been told this group probably wouldn't drink much. The funny thing was that when they saw the wine, they practically threw down their canes to get to it.

At the end of the afternoon, I saw two old gals sitting on my parents' front steps holding on to each other and laughing. It struck me how many gardeners are elderly. It must be that gardening helps you live longer. We were counting on its restorative powers ourselves. Mother had a month to convalesce from surgery on the green chaise longue backed by two arches covered in honeysuckle. By her side were pots of rose-scented geraniums at arm's reach so she could periodically run her fingers across them to release their perfume. I'm sure it helped.

August

Feast Days: First Day of Harvest, My Parents' Anniversary

The Naked Ladies are out, even along the highway. This is our favorite thing to tell friends because it startles them every time. Naked Ladies are a form of lily that have no leaves, hence the name. Sunflowers, cosmos, yarrow, dahlias, gladiolas (finally, though they were not very strong this year), ranunculus, phlox, and hollyhocks are also in bloom. The roses are in a brief lull, but I can't complain. We've had almost a continuous bloom of roses this year, especially up at the corral. Mother's summer table decoration has been Mint Julep roses—the pale green kind with a thin pink trim—in Swedish cobalt blue glass vases down the center of the table, surrounded by her collection of single antique crystal candlesticks. Some days she mixes in a few bright yellow and red nasturtiums, which look charming and serve a double purpose, since we can nibble on them if we get hungry.

For "real" vegetables, we have broccoli, cauliflower, runner beans, beets, fennel—which I love with Sauvignon Blanc—potatoes, eggplant, more zucchini, peppers, and beautiful lettuce. It's the season for crudités and pepper oil. We often eat nothing but corn for dinner in August. We put the water on to boil before the corn is even picked. It's so fresh and sweet it doesn't need any butter and tastes delicious with Chardonnay.

We have 5 acres of wild blackberries and the most gorgeous peaches. Mother picks the peaches herself. She says no one else does it quite right. You have to be slow and methodical. They can bruise from the tree to the kitchen. The white Babcocks are the most fragile. Mom gives them as hostess gifts. She'll sit in the car holding the basket on her lap as if they were made of crystal.

August 3. I love Forrest's food best of all. He created a variation on shrimp Louis for me today: cooked baby shrimp tossed in Louis sauce, and a thin slice of avocado between two slices of Marvel Stripe tomatoes. He makes the dressing with three tablespoons of Pavel's Russian Style Yogurt, one tablespoon of ketchup, a splash of Worchestershire, a dash of Tabasco, and a lemon squeeze. We drank a bottle of German Riesling, which was a gift to us from Peter Granoff, aka "cork dork"—a master sommelier, one of a handful of Americans to pass this rigorous British test on wine and wine service. He now has a "storefront" on the Internet, Virtual Vineyards (http://www.virtualvin.com), selling specialty wine in cyberspace. The bottle he gave us was a 1991 Nackenheimer Rothenberg Spätlese Trocken, a small family estate in the Reinhessen. Nackenheim is the village, Rothenberg the name of the vineyard, considered the best in the village, which is named for the reddish sandy loam soil. *Spätlese Trocken* means a little less sweet—less than 1 percent residual sugar. Many *trocken* wines from Germany are dry to the point of severity, but this one was exceptional for its gorgeous fruit. It was both floral and minerally with notes of honey, delicate orange blossoms, and peaches. It just glided across the tongue and tasted all the more exotic with Cavaillon melon for dessert.

August 12. Lunch for Stella Fishback, Charlie Trotter, et al. This lunch was important to my mother. Mrs. Fishback is someone she admires tremendously, who, at eighty-four, was walking up and down our hills so fast she had everyone else running after her. And, having Charlie Trotter, one of Chicago's star restaurateurs, to lunch begs the question "What do you serve a chef?"

Lunch was outside, but Mother wanted to make it one of her best table settings. She threw a soft hand-painted cloth over the table, used white-and-gilt porcelain dinner plates, old-fashioned silver, and crystal wine glasses to create an Impressionist scene.

The menu had lots of vegetables up front—French beans, cherry tomatoes both yellow and red, and candy striped beets in a light peanut oil sauce served with Brut Rosé. Lobster consommé was served warm with a

Fumé Blanc and a prize-winning lamb from the Sonoma County Fair with Pinot Noir. Salad greens, country bread, and a selection of cheeses with Cabernet. Sliced peaches and Demi-Sec. One of the guests, Steve Greystone, said he would remember this lunch for the best peach he ever ate.

The Demi-Sec is my father's creation. Ours is actually at the low end of Demi-Sec. The scale of sweetness of champagnes and sparklings is specified by Common Market regulations. Brut may contain between 0.5 to 1.5 percent residual sugar, extra dry from 1.2 to 2 percent sugar, and demi-sec from 3.5 to 5 percent sugar. One of the schisms in the nomenclature between California and France is that we use the word "brut" also to mean a blend of Pinot Noir and Chardonnay, as opposed to our Blancs de Blancs and Blancs de Noirs, though they are all equally dry. In fact, one of the technical differences between California sparklings and most champagnes is that ours are drier. We can balance the wines naturally with fruit instead of loading it with sugar at the end of the process. I have wanted to name our Demi-Sec "Cuvée Barry Sterling," but Father says no. I can't decide if he's being modest or if he really hates the idea.

August 16. Mark and I attended the Fourth Annual Sonoma Cheese Festival—a goat-cheese tasting that took place during the national cheese makers' convention held in Sonoma this year. Each cheese producer was matched up with a chef and a winery. The chef at

John Ash, Jeffrey Madura, prepared a goat cheese and lemon thyme crème brûlée. Since the tasting was outdoors, in a walnut grove, the only way he could caramelize the tops was with a mini propane blowtorch.

Mark prepared a cheesecake, using Cindy Calahan's sheep's milk ricotta, golden raisins, and almonds, and it was delicious with Brut.

He made the cake by first warming a quarter cup of Vin Santo and pouring it over a half cup of golden raisins. Vin Santo is made from Muscat grapes and used to be associated with the monasteries. The next step of this recipe is to toast a half cup of pine nuts over medium heat in a skillet until lightly brown. Then, four cups of Bellwether Farms sheep's milk ricotta, one cup of heavy cream, four large eggs (preferably duck eggs), and six tablespoons of sugar go into a bowl and are whisked for a few minutes until well blended. Then the raisins, wine, and pine nuts are added and stirred together. The mixture is spooned into an eight-inch springform pan lined with parchment paper, placed on a baking sheet with a half inch of water, and baked at 375 degrees for an hour and a quarter to an hour and a half. The cake is cooled on a rack before being removed from the pan, and is served at room temperature, garnished with three cups of peeled and sliced white peaches.

This is a cheesecake to be eaten the same day it's made, unlike a cream cheese cake, which can be refrigerated. It goes with Brut because the recipe is not too sweet. I recommend Demi-Sec for more sugary desserts. One "rule" of food and wine pairing, which proves correct nine out of ten times, is that the dish should never be sweeter than the wine.

Surprisingly, not all cheeses taste good to me with sparkling. I like fresh, mild goat cheese, Parmesan, which is a classic combination in Champagne, and ricotta, which, with a glass of sparkling, can be dessert with the simple addition of sliced peaches or wild blackberries.

One of Forrest's current favorite cheese and wine combinations is a very grassy Sauvignon Blanc with a piece of tangy Jarlsberg. Sheep's milk cheeses and rosato de Sangiovese are perfect together. Aged cheeses like Brie and triple crèmes like St. André are best with aged reds. We like aged chèvre like Topinaire with older Cabernet. We often serve Vella dried jack with Cabernet, and for Laurence's birthday one year we had Gorgonzola with honey and toasted almonds and 1963 Fonseca Port.

My father's idea of formal dining necessarily includes cheese. He says he remembers very distinctly the day he discovered Laura Chenel chèvre and the feeling that civilization had finally arrived in Sonoma County. Laurie is considered the "grande dame" of California cheese. She used to tell the story that when she traveled to Europe to learn, the French cheesemakers wouldn't let her in, saying it was bad enough that we make wine in California, but cheese was going too far. She also taught us that one of the problems with the cheese business is that goats naturally lactate in August, when unfortunately demand for cheese is at its lowest. Apparently they have to be coaxed into lactating in December when the market is stronger, which conjured up images of Laurie wearing a bikini and dark glasses in the middle of winter to fool the goats.

There are now twenty-two cheesemakers in Sonoma. Some are neighbors. In fact, one of the controversies of the summer was the goat house under construction right up against our property line, in the middle of one of our favorite views—looking up at the vineyards to the west. Actually, now what we see is the aluminum siding of a refrigerated walk-in where our new neighbors plan to store and age their cheeses. Presumably the goats will be housed on the other side of the building.

Our recourse was to plant twelve coastal redwoods, which will eventually hide the goat house. It will take a while—the trees are in 5-gallon cans. The owner of the nursery said they will be 10 feet tall next year and will grow 3 to 6 feet a year. And no one would dare cut down a redwood.

August 26. First day of harvest. It's already starting to look like fall, or at least the start of the transition period to fall. There's a slight but noticeable shift in the colors, the angle of the sun is different, the light seems softer, the days are definitely shorter, and the fragrances are different. Iron Horse smells like golden hay. It's a distinctly Sonoma scent of dry hills. And you can catch the smell of grapes in the air. It's an odor that becomes more intense as the grapes ripen, like an apple orchard at its harvest time. I asked Forrest if he was excited about starting to pick grapes and he surprised me by saying no, not really, because he spends all year trying to get grapes on the vine, so it's a little upsetting now to just pull them off.

So far, the vintage has been completely unpredictable. We've had no fog all August, which is odd, because fog is one of Iron Horse's identifying features. The difference has been noticeable; we've had dinner outside more nights this summer than any other year I can remember. Usually it's quite cool by sundown and there's a wall of fog waiting in the wings to slowly march across the property. It comes in from the south, through the Petaluma gap in the coastal range. The fog blankets the property in the wee hours and by daybreak it's 45 degrees and the air is drippingly moist. I think of the fog as one of the defining elements of our vineyard and consequently our style of wine. And yet, contrary to what I would have expected, this has not been a hot, fast vintage. We're starting harvest at the normal time—over three months since bud break—which means it has been a nice, long growing season. The temperature drops at night, cooling off the vineyard and prolonging the ripening process, but, without the fog, it drops more slowly and politely waits until after dinner.

August 27. Dinner for a family friend. This was an advance celebration of Matt Byrne's birthday and the only chance we'd have because of everyone's traveling schedule. We never feel it's necessary to celebrate a birthday or any holiday on the exact day. It's more important for everyone to be together when they can.

For this occasion, Mark prepared ballottine of pheasant to go with reserve Chardonnay in magnums. The main course was venison and garden vegetables, served with 1992 Merlot. It was surprising to have game so early in the year, kind of like seeing football on television and thinking it's too soon.

The pheasant was boned. The filling was pheasant legs ground with apple wood–smoked bacon, heavy cream, nutmeg, allspice, and fresh bread crumbs. Pheasant goes with Chardonnay because it's light meat and the apple and vanilla flavors of the wine are traditionally associated with this bird.

"Reserve" on a wine label should mean something, but the word has been worn thin by low-quality wines. The best of swill is sometimes called reserve.

One of the benefits of magnums is that wine ages more slowly in the bigger bottle. Magnums are very festive and practical for a table of six or more when you are going to need that much to go around.

The venison came from New Zealand. (Okay, so we're not always virtuous.) The Merlot, though, was from T-bar-T. This is our first crop from 4 acres Forrest planted in 1989.

Merlot is *the* wine of the moment. There isn't a drop to be had on the bulk market. Our distributors say they can't hold on to it. Waiters claim people order it without even knowing what they're drinking. The generally accepted explanation is that Merlot is more luscious and easier to drink than Cabernet Sauvignon. It is less tannic, softer, much more approachable when young. Some connoisseurs say they order Merlot in restaurants when the Cabernets on the list are too young. Others think it is just a current phase in the fashion cycle.

The interesting thing to me about Merlot is that it is selling like crazy and yet for many connoisseurs it is not their favorite grape. Cabernet Sauvignon or Pinot Noir would take that honor. One notable exception is Christian Moueix, whose Pétrus, one of the most expensive and sought-after wines in the world, is predominantly Merlot.

All wines are subject to fashion. When was the last time anyone offered you a sherry, or a German wine? Zinfandel goes in and out of style and at its low points is made into white Zinfandel. California Chardonnays have undergone drastic swings in the last thirty years. There are times when even the bubbles of champagne are démodé. Swizzle sticks, which were all the rage from the 1930s through the '60s, were just a fancy means of stirring up the wine to kill the bubbles.

Zinfandel fell out of style in the '70s because the wine was being made in such a way that the only food you could imagine eating them with was raw game. The winemakers seemed to be competing over who could make the biggest, toughest, most tannic and alcoholic rendition.

California Chardonnay has gone from being an uncomplicated white wine in the mid to late '60s (no barrel fermentation, no malolactic fermentation, no wood aging) to the '70s, when big, buttery, and oaky were mainstream requirements. The dictum for the '80s was harmonious, elegant, and food enhancing.

Today, every style is out there, but trends are emerging. One is sweetness. Many more California Chardonnays than one would expect are discernibly sweet — Forrest guesses about 60 percent. Sugar can take the edge off a wine, smooth it out. It can add texture and weight. It can be used as a technique for covering up some of the hardness that comes from overpressing. It tends to yield a more consistent product and, as Forrest says, can mask a multitude of sins. Some experts contend that "American taste" is synonymous with sweet.

Food is a very important force in the evolution of wine. How we eat greatly determines the kind of wine we want to drink. This is certainly true in France, where wines were made to accompany butter and cream. Traditionally, Bordeaux food is very plain, to show off the wines. Now, the growing use of vegetables, olive oil, and aromatic spices has led chefs to seek out wines more in the "California style," with more zing and fruit. In America, higher standards for freshness and quality naturally lead to more interest in wine. In North Dakota, for example, three local talents who attended the Culinary Institute of America in Hyde Park, New York, have now come home to open restaurants, and the result is a food and wine festival in the Badlands attended by Justin Meyer of Silver Oak winery. Likewise, the burgeoning phenomenon of Hawaiian regional cuisine has made the Islands a growing wine market, especially for sparkling, Viognier and Sangiovese, which taste especially delicious with the local flavors.

Another factor in setting wine styles is the media. *The Wine Spectator* and Robert Parker have defined certain styles of wine, which they rate as 90 and above, and more than one winemaker has confessed to making wines that conform to the ratings system. The operative words for highly rated wines are "big" and "opulent," though I have noticed that the word "delicate" has slipped into a few descriptions in *The Spectator* and Parker lately.

Wines can mirror the tastes of the day and they can be slaves to the vagaries of fashion. Fortunately there are still wines of passion, wines that defy fashion, and they probably account for about 5 percent of the wines being produced today.

Sunday, August 28. Lunch at our house today was about the best I've had in a long time. It helped that we had yesterday's leftover ballottine of pheasant, and Forrest prepared four beautiful garden salads to go with it. He made perfectly steamed broccoli with pine nuts in a light sesame oil dressing; and a selection of sliced tomatoes and basil—beefsteaks, Marvel Stripes, which are big and variegated, red and yellow cherries, and yellow Russians, which are very sweet and look like persimmons. He put together a bowl of baby greens, the first of the new crop, with just a few drops of fine olive oil and balsamic vinegar. The fourth salad was

French beans sautéd with onions and chanterelles, still slightly crisp and served at room temperature. We had two kinds of cheeses: Cindy Callahan's smoked sheep's milk, and a white, creamy Teleme. This was a one-course meal, served buffet style, but with two wines— 1993 Fumé Blanc and 1992 Cuvée R, a light Pinot Noir served slightly chilled, which, when we switched from the white to the red, had a nice way of breaking up the meal and comfortably extending it without adding more courses.

September

Feast Days: Harvest Lunches, Labor Day

September 1. First day of Harvest Lunch. Some wineries shut their doors during harvest because it's so hectic, but we do the opposite. We invite all our friends and customers to come for lunch.

We have cut down the number of weeks and increased the number of people we will entertain for harvest lunch this year. We plan to welcome forty guests a day—not counting family and winery crew—five days a week for five weeks. Mommy just laughs when one of her friends takes to her bed after a dinner party for twelve.

My mother feels there's no more work involved in entertaining eight people than one and that the same amount of effort goes into entertaining sixteen as fifty.

The mise-en-scène for harvest lunch begins with the pick list. This is when we eat up everything in the garden. One of the responsibilities of having a kitchen garden is that you must plan your menus around what's ripe and most abundant. Right now we're knee deep in tomatoes, eggplants, and peppers, the exciting vegetables that Father picks himself. The rosemary growing rampant in the corral is so pungent now that sometimes the resinous smell of it is overwhelming. For dessert there are melons, table grapes, and figs.

About a week before the harvest lunches begin, Mother takes out and counts service for sixty, which will later get carted down to the gazebo behind the winery every day, then back up to the Big House to be washed in the afternoon.

The gazebo is dropped down a few steps below the main winery building on the far north side, facing the vineyards. There are four heavily laden apple trees, a giant floribunda interwound in the wood slates of the gazebo, several pale pink climbers in the inside corners, and pots of ivy and geraniums on every table.

Shirley Everly sets the tables in between weighing loads of grapes. We use long picnic tables and benches painted wine red like the winery, white faience dishes with the Iron Horse logo in the same Cabernet red, paper napkins stamped with the rampant horse, hammered stainless-steel place settings, three all-purpose glasses at each place—two for wine and one for water— also bearing our symbol. Everywhere you look are iron horses. The very first iron horse was originally an old weathervane that we unearthed when we were leveling

the ground to build the winery. Now it's replicated everywhere. I see iron horses in my dreams.

By 10 A.M., my mother comes down to the winery to
check the plants, look back over that day's guest list,
and wipe down the benches one more time. She has six
people helping her, including Mark and the kitchen
staff, but harvest lunch, and in fact most of the entertaining at Iron Horse, is her job, and I have absolutely
no intention of letting her retire.

The scenario is for guests to arrive at noon. We serve
Brut in Iron Horse flutes while everyone assembles.
The only requirement for getting a glass is to sign the
guest book. My parents are rather insistent. Everyone
who has ever been here for a party has signed it. We
are now on volume three. I tell people it provides them
with an alibi in case they were plotting to rob a bank.

By 12:20 P.M., Father and Laurence start counting
heads and if the majority of the guests are there, Daddy
claps his hands together and announces he is going to
give a tour of the winery for those who are interested.
He insists it's not obligatory, but everyone really is expected to follow along. We go around topping off the
glasses. It's about a forty-minute loop. My father's tours
are very warm and personal. He's full of stories, and
the main thing you come away with is his passion for
Iron Horse. Forrest's tours usually run longer because
he's more serious and talks extensively about the vintage at hand. Laurence's are the shortest. They're
funny, but in a different way from Daddy's, because

Laurence has such a dry, English sense of humor. All are best with a glass of sparkling in hand.

Meanwhile, behind the scenes, Mark is roasting peppers up at the Big House, making brandade, or watching a confit simmer. My mom sits down on a bench in the gazebo. She is dressed in a soft, billowy caftan. She never wears a watch as a hostess because she doesn't want to look hurried or harried, but at five minutes to one o'clock she is instinctively drumming her fingers wondering, Where's Mark?

The work of harvest is going on all around. The grapes are coming in. The bins are stacked in the shade, buzzing with honeybees attracted to the sugar. We load the grapes into the presses as quickly as possible. Like every fruit and vegetable, grapes start to break down right after they're picked. You can see and taste the juice as it flows out of the presses. Hoses are everywhere, pumping the juice into tanks.

Mark arrives at the winery in an old brown and tan Suburban, vintage 1981, which never goes any farther than the mile's drive to Forestville anymore. The houseman is at the wheel. Emma, a part-time student who helps serve and wash dishes, is in front. Mark is riding with his legs hanging off the back end of the truck with the food loaded up behind him.

Philip slowly drives the Suburban through the traffic of forklifts to the gazebo. They quickly set up a buffet under an old olive tree with mosquito netting hanging down from one of the branches to keep the yellow jackets away from the meat. We also burn citronella candles to ward them off. Platters of roasted peppers and fresh, homemade cheese crostini, sliced tomatoes, and home-cured prosciutto are set on each table as antipasti, along with chunks of country bread, and opened bottles of each of the wines we produce are plunked down the middle of the table.

Sometimes Mark cuts it close, but for five years he has always managed to arrive just before Father emerges from the disgorging cellar and starts up the hill with a train of guests behind him. Every day, my mother snaps everyone in the gazebo to attention by saying, "It's showtime."

The people we invite to harvest lunch are a mix of friends and business acquaintances. It is like going to a wedding in the sense that you can talk to anyone. The common denominator is Iron Horse.

The menu changes daily. The entrées include lamb shanks and confit of duck. Forrest and I would love it if we could serve a vegetarian feast, but my parents feel the guests would find it lacking.

Brandade, which Mark prepares as an appetizer, is one of my favorite dishes. We serve it in a dish with a spoon or a knife so you can spread it on a slice of toast. It goes beautifully with a platter of red beets and al dente haricots verts.

Our brandade recipe calls for a pound of salt cod — boneless, skinless, preferably the center cut of the fish — to serve eight people. For two days, you have to soak the salt cod in a gallon of cold water in the refrigerator, changing the water twice daily. When ready to cook, put half the last soaking water and two bay leaves in a large pan, add the cod, bring to a boil, then remove the pan immediately from the heat. Let it stand for fifteen minutes.

Meanwhile, dice one large peeled boiling potato and put it in a small pot. Cover with water, add a pinch of salt, and cook until it's just tender. Let it cool and then mash it in a bowl. In separate pans, heat a cup of heavy cream and three cups of extra virgin olive oil over medium heat until both are warm. Remove the cod from the water and break it into small pieces. Discard the bay leaves. Pound four cloves of garlic in a mortar to a fine paste. Put the cod, the garlic paste, and the mashed potato in a food processor. Pulse, adding the warm oil a little at a time.

After the oil is added, the mixture should appear smooth. Add the warm cream. The cod should now have a fluffy texture. Place in a serving bowl, season with freshly ground black pepper, and drizzle with more olive oil.

As for the wines, people fend for themselves. Each one of the wines we produce is there for the taking, and you can try them one after another as the meal progresses. Sometimes there's a favorite wine with a particular dish, like Chardonnay with brandade or Pinot Noir with figs and prosciutto, but more often we taste everything that's offered regardless of the match. We have no qualms about throwing out on the gravel or in a flowerpot any amount of wine in a glass in order to be able to try another. The only rule of etiquette is to try not to splash the person next to you.

All of us in the family get up between courses to help clear plates and serve salad and cheese. On very hot days, we keep the Cabernets in the cool of the winery until this point in the meal so the wine won't cook in the sun. Father calls for everyone's attention, proposes a toast to the harvest, and graciously thanks everyone for bringing good weather, which is always the sign of a good guest. Then we all go up to my parents' home — a brief stroll down the row of palms and to the right along the edge of the orchard and the gardens — for dessert: fresh fruit, chocolate truffles, and coffee. At this point, it takes very little coaxing to get Daddy to give a brief garden tour. He points out the dahlias, Japanese anemones, and impatiens, ironically planted next to the obedience plants, scientifically named Physostegia, which get their common name because they stand perfectly straight. Even with the garden walk thrown in, all our guests are back in their cars and en route by 3 or 3:30.

I always enjoy harvest lunch, but then again, I start traveling on behalf of the winery the day after Labor Day, so I'm not home for most of the lunches. I don't know how Forrest, Laurence, and my parents do it. Mother missed only one harvest lunch this year because of her knee.

From watching my parents, I would say the keys to entertaining are forethought, planning, and attention to detail, right down to checking the bathrooms. "You laugh," says Mother. "But often it's the basics that get overlooked."

Entertaining requires that you be on your feet almost the whole time—first introducing the guests to one another, then helping them get seated, going around to the tables to make sure everyone is well situated and getting wine. It is the hosts' responsibility to make sure everyone's glass is full, and that conversation flows as well. Everyone should feel like an honored guest and it should all seem perfectly effortless.

As frequent hosts my parents have very firm opinions on what it takes to be a good guest. First is to respond to an invitation promptly. Second is to arrive at the party on time. Third is to come prepared with conversation. Everyone is expected to bring something to the table—be it wit, charm, or beauty. Being controversial is acceptable as long as you are not combative. If you are at a loss, the wine provides a common ground. I'm sure this is why it has always been the drink of diplomats. Even if you can't agree on sex, politics, or religion, you can always talk about the wine.

Another attribute of a good guest is to notify your hosts of any dietary restrictions in advance. It causes more trouble if you wait until you are seated to mention that you are a vegetarian or allergic to fish.

My father feels adaptability is important in a guest— you have to fit into the hosts' milieu. Finally, a good guest knows when to leave. In my mother's view, a great lunch lasts two and a half hours. Dinner, three.

She says even the best party can only sustain so much fun for four hours maximum.

Sunday, September 4. Labor Day weekend. Jeff Dawson's annual garden party. Jeff manages the organic vegetable gardens at Fetzer Vineyards in Mendocino, and he is designing the kitchen gardens for the Culinary Institute of America's California branch in Napa. He leases 5 acres from us on the east side of the creek, where he raises produce for restaurants such as Postrio, Larkcreek Inn, and One Market. We enjoy kind of a sharecropping arrangement with him. We have liberal picking rights and when our supply is simply overwhelming, he helps by selling it on our behalf in the city.

There's little or no replication between Jeff's garden and Father's. Most of Jeff's vegetables are seed-saver varieties that were on the verge of extinction until a few groups started saving and trading seeds to keep them in production.

Every year for his party Jeff sets up a couple of folding tables between the rows of tomatoes and peppers in his section of the garden. This time the garden party menu was abalone on mashed potatoes with garlic, Iron Horse tomatoes, very lightly dressed mâche, grilled corn with lime, and California sea bass in a Chinese marinade (rice wine, soy sauce, fresh cilantro, and scallions) grilled over broken, purple-stained wine barrel staves, and served with peppers and eggplant and garlic cooked into a kind of ratatouille. There were three kinds of peppers in this dish. And for dessert, a melon tasting—Red Queen, Orange Blossom, and Passion, all hybrids of cantaloupe, and Honey Brew, a very, very sweet honeydew. Jeff's favorite was the Red Queen. Mine was the Honey Brew.

The preparations for Jeff's garden parties start at around 4 P.M. I was quite delighted to see one of the guests/chefs pounding the abalone with a wine bottle. It is usually done with a hammer or the old-fashioned tools that were used to make Swiss steak. It's a tremendous treat to have abalone at a dinner party. It's strictly allocated to sportsfishing only, and the sportsmen who dive for abalone aren't allowed to use oxygen tanks. They have to go down about 20 feet, search for the mollusk in the undulating kelp, and practically pry off the meat with a crowbar, possibly against the current, in 46-degree water, always alert to the danger of a great white. They can't sell their catch legally. Consequently there's a thriving black market for wild abalone. Much of the farmed abalone is shipped to Japan. They are grown until they are six to eight years old, and sell wholesale for between 36 to 44 dollars per abalone; in Japan they retail for 115 dollars each.

The tables were littered with opened bottles of unlabeled, organic Viognier and Chardonnay from Fetzer, Jeff's homemade Cabernet, 1992 T-bar-T Merlot and, for me, Brut Rosé, which I gladly shared throughout.

"Organic" is a political word in California. More and more of our customers are asking about it and, in fact, viticulture leads the way for every kind of agriculture in moving from chemical-based farming, vintage 1970, to a more natural way of sustainable agriculture, vintage 1995. Fetzer Vineyards, which has committed to growing 100 percent of their grapes organically by the year 2000, is now within 75 percent of their goal. One of the largest table grape growers in California, Pandol Farms, is completely organic. The Robert Mondavi Winery is slowly converting its growers.

The most fascinating aspect of what we call "natural farming" is that it is both timeless and new. Many of the "new" practices, which we call "sustainable agriculture," and which we see as an evolution, were standard two generations ago. Sustainable agriculture was the norm. For example, we are now tying the vine canes to the trellising wires with twine—as opposed to Mylar—because twine is biodegradable. The antidote for mildew is soap and water. We use compost instead of commercial fertilizer in the vineyard, and we grow cover crops that attract bugs to them instead of to the vines.

Organic wine means no added sulfites, which reduces the shelf life. It can also mean that the winemaker uses no commercially produced materials in the winemaking relying on wild yeasts for fermentation and not using fining agents like bentonite, a special clay from Wyoming which sometimes results in wines that aren't that good.

Organically farmed grapes have to be certified by the CCOF, California Certified Organic Farmers, a governing board modeled after the Milk Council, which sets the standards for what qualifies as organic. All of our vegetables are grown organically, though we have never bothered to apply for certification. Forrest is loath to do so for the grapes because, even though the certification may have some marketing value, the board is another bureaucracy, which he prefers to avoid.

The 1990 California Organic Food Act includes some practices that Forrest feels are too lenient, and others—like forbidding the use of recycled winery water on the grapes or vegetables—that he thinks are absurd. "There isn't any reason," he says. "Winery wash water is a natural by-product, but in a regulatory sense it gets lumped in with every kind of waste water."

The way we farm is called "natural farming," which the French tout as *"biodynamique."* It involves more and earlier leaf pulling, beginning in June—we used to wait until July or August—which directs the energy of the vine from the very beginning into the grapes and not into growing leaves. We now start hedging, cutting back the vine canes, in June as well, letting more sunlight filter through to the grapes. Forrest's big experiment this year is going to be with different cover crops to feed the soil. He also plans to try some very simple organic fungicides and a seaweed fertilizer in addition to compost, lime, and gypsum. He's not using any herbicides. Where we have a weed problem he uses a fancy tractor plow. One of the advantages in California is that with our benign climate we can get away without using 90 percent of the commercial products that are necessary in other places because they have humidity and bugs.

In the long run, natural farming may even prove to

be more economical. Not just in terms of costs—chemical products are expensive and possibly no more useful than doing absolutely nothing, or trying something cultural like hedging, leaf pulling, or planting prune trees to host a predator wasp—but also in terms of keeping the land productive.

There's a small library on this topic, much of it quoting Thoreau in essays like "Good Farming in the Public Good" about preserving the land in the best possible way—what Forrest calls "stewardship" of the land. The concept is a holdover of traditions that go back forever, but unlike the family who owned the 2,000 acres that originally comprised Iron Horse, we cannot keep this place going on two cows, sixty chickens, fifty head of sheep, one hundred fruit trees, and a hundred varieties of tomatoes. That world disappeared in California around the time of World War II. Sustainable agriculture also means being able to stay in business.

What used to be a way of life is practically a political movement today. The issue, at least here in California, is a legitimate cause. Sometimes it feels as though California is no longer interested in being an agricultural state. Fewer people care whether we grow our own produce or fly it in from Chile, which to me, as a Californian, is very sad. This is why I tell people, "You have no idea how politically correct it is to buy California wine."

September 19. We are halfway through harvest in terms of tonnage. We've picked all the grapes for sparkling.

Today it is hot and windy, which Forrest calls "grape-ripening weather." That and forest fires is about all it's good for. The degree of sugar in the grapes will jump about a half point a day.

Mommy has changed the decorations on her dining room table. "We've put on our fall dress," she says. It is an abundant still life with autumn leaves, apples, and squash down the middle of the table, mixed with a nineteenth-century bunch of jade grapes and real clusters of Pinot Noir from the vineyard.

October

Feast Days: Father's Birthday, Halloween

Saturday, October 2. We picked a full bin of apples but couldn't get it pressed commercially because it was too small a load. However, this didn't deter us from making our own apple juice. José simply rented a hand-cranked wooden press. He had a plastic funnel to drain into 1-gallon jugs. It took two men two days to make 40 gallons that will last the family until the next crop. Of course, it all has to be frozen or it will start fermenting in three days and we'd be in the cider business.

The tomatoes are at their height. Forrest is canning his "special sauce." His recipe calls for a basketful of garden vegetables—three or four red onions, two green peppers, six baby eggplants, six cloves of garlic, two dozen small to medium size tomatoes, and two generous handfuls of fresh basil. He chops the onions, peppers, eggplants, and garlic, and sautés them all in olive oil until they're soft. He quickly quarters the tomatoes, chops the basil, and adds them to the pot. He lets the mixture slowly cook down, then strains it through a food mill, so it's just the essence of the vegetables.

Meanwhile, at the Big House, Father is making cornichons and Mark is freezing whole tomatoes. He lays them out on a tray or an empty shelf in the freezer so they're not touching. It takes about four hours to freeze them and then you can put them in bags. The nice thing about them is that when they thaw out the skins peel right off.

The red, yellow, and orange peppers are at perfection. We have enough Brussels sprouts to pay a college tuition. There are 100 pumpkins in the barn and at least another 100 in the field. Every kind of squash is being stored in the barn. And there are hundreds of bunches of dried peppers hanging from the rafters along with ornamental corn.

Hydrangeas, purple and rust-colored chrysanthemums, Japanese maples, ginkgo trees, liquid amber, and pyracanthus berries, both red and orange, provide the spectrum of autumn colors. The last of the dahlias are ready to be cut back. The sunflowers have been cut down; they're lying by the side of the garden. We still have enough cosmos and roses to fill several vases.

This is turning into an exceptionally long growing season. Forrest is becoming more excited about the vintage with each passing day because the longer the grapes stay on the vine, the more flavor they accumulate. We picked a little over 8 tons of Pinot Noir from block N, behind the corral. And then Forrest decided to stop for a few days.

The fermentation smells are beginning to build up in the winery. Fermentation has its own perfume. It smells like yeast, mixed with passion fruit, guava, pineapple, and ripe apple in Sauvignon Blanc and Viognier; banana, apple, and citrus in Chardonnay. The reds smell like black fruit. Cabernet particularly has a very strong smell of black currant, black cherry, blackberry, sometimes ripe plum. The escaping carbon dioxide liberates all these smells and brings them up into your nose.

The winery this time of year is cold and damp. We keep our cellars at 55 degrees and 90 percent humidity. Our winery is built of wood, which accentuates the smell of the newly filled barrels.

You can put your ear to a barrel and hear fermentation. It's like listening to the ocean in a shell. The juice inside is bubbling from the center of the barrel up to the top. You can hear it working its magic, turning grape juice into wine.

This has been one of those interesting harvests when the grapes have ripened and matured at different times. They are still a ways from what Forrest calls "that true point of interest." That is a far cry from where they were just a month ago. Then Forrest was convinced that we were having a 1984 type of year, with early ripening, plummy fruit and very good wine, but none of us think of that vintage as a great year at Iron Horse. A great year has a different flavor profile. It has more depth and complexity, like an accordion opening up to produce more notes.

At first Forrest said he would pick Chardonnay on Monday. Now he's waiting till Tuesday—even with Father asking him repeatedly, "When are you going to pick? What's the sugar?" Chardonnay is our cash crop. On top of which, Forrest has to fend off his own desire to "get it in" instead of waiting for that "perfect moment."

We walked through Block B, one of our favorite blocks for Chardonnay still wine, tasting the grapes along the rows. It was a perfect fall day. The afternoon sun seemed to glow in the vineyard, especially among the Chardonnay, which has turned from green to golden.

I asked Forrest what the difference will be in two days. He said the sugar won't change, at least not enough to matter, so it's not a question of "ripeness," but that the flavors will be more intense. "Don't get me wrong," he said, "this will make very good wine, but 'good' isn't good enough around here. At least that's what everybody tells me."

Tuesday, October 4. My heart sank as it started to rain. We have 100 tons of Chardonnay, about 12 tons of Pinot Noir, and another 20 tons of Cabernet still out on the vine. "That's farming," said Forrest. He has no choice but to tough it out, but I can tell you, that night he didn't really feel like talking to anyone. He said he just wanted to hide under the covers.

It turned out that the rain was just an exhausting twenty-four hours of self-doubt and panic. It didn't damage even the tomatoes. The next day was Indian summer. We had to wait another two days to resume picking, as the grapes were full of water, diluting the flavors. With luck, by Friday, we'll be back to where we were.

Thursday, October 6. I was in Louisville as part of a selling spree and for a winemaker dinner at Equus. The very talented chef designed a five-course dinner with a different wine specifically chosen for each course. One dish involved three kinds of mushrooms, each prepared a different way, served with Pinot Noir. This was followed by London broil with sun-dried Michigan cherries and white truffle oil for the main course, a perfect match with the Cabernets, bringing out all its fruit, but which frankly made the Pinot taste somewhat tannic — hard, bitter, and astringent. This showed the fallacy of my libertine or laissez-faire attitude about wine and food. Sometimes, perhaps even often, one wine *is* in fact better than another. There's only one way to know these things and that is to experiment and bear in mind that there isn't just one choice.

Saturday, October 8. We picked Chardonnay yesterday and today. We'll stop again tomorrow. Forrest wants to consolidate what we already have in and resume harvesting on Monday. There's still about sixty tons of

Chardonnay on the vine plus the remaining Pinot and Cabernet.

Tuesday, October 11. One day it's hot and the next it's foggy and cloudy with rain forecast for Saturday. Now Forrest wants to get it all in or we'll be harvesting at Christmas.

Saturday, October 15. The last day of harvest and the last day of Harvest Lunch. Everyone is very excited about both. Mark prepared confit of duck for the occasion.

There are four steps to making confit. It is the epitome of slow cooking. You first rub duck legs with salt, herbs, and spices, store and refrigerate for twelve to fourteen hours or longer, taking into consideration the overall size and thickness of the meat. The reason for this step, aside from flavoring the duck, is that the salt extracts moisture. The more moisture extracted, the longer the confit will keep.

The next step is to cook the meat. This is done by placing the duck in rendered duck fat and cooking over low heat for two or three hours. If need be, you can start the legs in two cups of pure olive oil to render enough fat out of the legs to get your confit going. Do not let the fat come to a boil, just a nice gentle simmer.

The third step is to store the confit. Mark likes to put it in a large sterilized earthenware or glass bowl. Confit should be aged at least a week in a cool place and it can be kept several months.

When you are ready to serve it, take the container out of the refrigerator and let the fat come to room temperature, making it easier to remove the duck. Wipe off the excess fat, heat in oven to warm meat, and place under a broiler to crisp the skin.

Duck Confit

Serves 8

Ingredients:

8 Moulard or Muscovy duck legs, approx. 6 to 8 pounds
5 tablespoons sea salt
1 tablespoon black peppercorns, crushed
1 small bunch fresh thyme
2 bay leaves, crushed
¼ teaspoon crushed allspice
½ teaspoon nutmeg grated
12 cloves of garlic, peeled
6 cloves
8 cups rendered duck fat

Directions:

Place the duck legs in a large mixing bowl with the salt, peppercorns, thyme, bay leaves, allspice, and nutmeg. Rub well with mixture. Lightly crush the garlic and toss in with the cloves. Cover the bowl and refrigerate for twenty-four hours.

In a heavy casserole or Dutch oven melt the rendered

duck fat over medium-low heat. Take the duck legs out of the refrigerator, wipe off the herbs, spices, and salt and dry thoroughly. Add the duck pieces and garlic to the fat and let simmer. After two to three hours, the meat should fall off when pierced. Remove from the pot and place in sterilized jars, or earthenware containers. Pour the duck fat through a very fine strainer or slotted spoon to cover the duck. Cool to room temperature, and then refrigerate for at least a week.

When you are ready to eat the confit, remove from the refrigerator, bring to room temperature, and wipe off excess fat. The confit is ready to use for a variety of recipes with beans, salads, potatoes, stews, soups, or even sandwiches.

Tuesday, October 25. We celebrated Father's sixty-fifth birthday in New York with dinner at Aureole. The meal was rich and flavorful, an all-American extravaganza.

As we sipped the wines, especially the 1982 Cabernets, it struck all of us for the first time that we now have enough history to be able to pick special vintages of our own wines instead of reaching into my father's French cellar for major celebrations. The mature bouquet and touch of nuttiness and richness of our Chardonnay as it gets older complemented the lobster dish, especially because of the citrusy undertones in the wine's lingering finish. Pepper-seared tuna and Pinot Noir is a classic combination. Pheasant is dense and strong, and this dish had a lovely autumn sweetness to it, which matched the fruit of the Cabernet. I think

DINNER CELEBRATION FOR BARRY STERLING

October 25, 1994

Hors d'Oeuvre for Champagne
Iron Horse, Brut, Late Disgorged, 1987

◆ ◆ ◆

Warm Autumn Lobster Salad with Citrus Leeks
Iron Horse, Chardonnay, 1990

◆ ◆ ◆

Pepper Seared Tuna with Toasted Barley Risotto
balsamic glaze and roasted beet jus

Iron Horse, Pinot Noir, 1986

◆ ◆ ◆

"Cleari Farm" Pheasant with Truffled White Bean Ravioli
a braise of Oregon chanterelles and two cabbages

Iron Horse, Cabernet Sauvignon, 1982

◆ ◆ ◆

Warm Aureole Apple Pudding with Sour Cream Ice Cream
honey spiced apple compote, clear caramel and vanilla crisps

Iron Horse, Demi-Sec, 1990

◆ ◆ ◆

Hand-made Chocolates, Fancied Fruits and Crisp Cookies
"Audrey" Brandy & "Joie de Vie" Liqueur

Aureole   34 East 61st Street   10021   212-319-1660

drinking this vintage was particularly gratifying for my father. We all felt a sense of accomplishment.

My dad started collecting wine in 1957, shortly after Laurence was born. We had moved into a new house and my parents were beginning to entertain at home.

Since then two basic factors have changed. First, wines are much more costly. Secondly, wines the world over are made to be drunk when they're young instead of after extensive aging in a personal cellar. Daddy's cellar book shows many examples of wines like Pétrus, Aussone, and Haut-Brion which he bought for less than $20 a bottle. The money was worth more then, but even factoring in inflation it was still sensible to buy such wines, enjoy them freely, and keep a few bottles for thirty years to see what would happen. Now, we and the world over have developed a taste for young wines. Ninety-five percent of all wine is consumed the day it is purchased.

A wine cellar can begin innocently enough as a rack in the kitchen or a hallway closet. Even the White House cellar is just a small pantry off the downstairs kitchen where a few cases can be stored. My father's cellar is a small, locked room that's a perfect mess. Cases are stacked all over the floor, so you can barely walk in. This is where we store Iron Horse wines that have become very low in inventory at the winery. They're safer there, in the sense that even I won't sell something from Daddy's cellar.

Some wine collectors are speculators. They buy rare and expensive wine with the aim of selling it at a later date for profit. Another kind of collector buys expensive wine, or did for a long period of time, and then either loses interest or feels it's too valuable to drink. Having reached the enviable point of being able to afford Château Latour, they feel unable to uncork it.

The main reason for starting a cellar is to have wine on hand to enjoy spontaneously. Another reason is to snap up wines in limited supply when they're available, so you buy more than will be immediately consumed. This also allows you to taste how a wine develops with age. A bottle here, a magnum there. Pretty soon, we're talking about a collection. The idea behind buying a case is to watch a wine develop. Wine is a living, breathing thing. It changes with time.

There's always a certain amount of heartbreak involved with wine. A bottle can go over the hill, or it can be corked—which means it has been spoiled by a bad cork, or, for no apparent reason, a wine just doesn't show very well on some days.

A very simplistic explanation of what happens to a red wine as it ages is that the tannins soften, and the fruit slowly fades, replaced by a different bouquet, special smells that come only with time. Chardonnays tend to mature in a linear way. What you taste in a young wine becomes more intense with time, and the acidity seems to diminish. Cabernet-based wines go through many gyrations, but generally speaking, phenolic compounds—volatile esters, tannins and coloring components—all react with each other in the bottle. The higher the concentration of each of these components, in balanced proportions, the longer the wine can continue to evolve. That's what aging potential means.

Chemically, over an extensive period of time, the small phenolic compounds form larger, more complex polymers. As they link up they make new components that smell slightly different. Eventually, these long chains of molecules become so heavy they exceed their solubility and drop out as dark, reddish-brown sediment, leaving a softer, gentler wine. At the same time there are further, much more complicated and much less well understood processes that gradually change the hue of the wine and its bouquet.

The current theory is that the small amount of oxygen in the bottle, in the "air space" between the cork and the wine, is bound up relatively quickly—from a few days to a few weeks after bottling—and that what is going on inside the bottle occurs under reductive conditions. The limited amount of oxygen gets transferred from compound to compound, none of them very stable. As some compounds lose their oxygen—are reduced—others acquire it—are oxidized—and a whole new array of esters is being formed from complex combinations of acids and alcohols.

Fortunately, how wine ages is still not perfectly defined. There's no way to scientifically pinpoint when a wine will reach its peak, or someone would have found a way to replicate the desired effects without having to wait. The important idea is to taste the wine when its young, then try a bottle a year or so later, then another bottle in three years, and on until that sad day when it's gone. A cellar book serves as a diary where, besides keeping an inventory, you can also jot down tasting notes and read how the wines have evolved. Keeping it up requires some discipline. My father's cellar book hasn't been updated since Forrest and I reorganized his cellar as a birthday present eight years ago, and I'm afraid it's woefully in need of it again.

At a certain point in life, most collectors start to slow down their acquisitions. André Simon, who wrote more than 100 books on wine and the wine industry, worried that he would never be able to drink all the wines he had collected. He set to the task in his mid-seventies and died at ninety-three with only one bottle left in his cellar.

Friday, October 28. The main attraction of my job is that I eat and drink very glamorously. I save special menus and have compiled an impressive collection.

One of my favorites lunches was held a year ago in the private dining room of our wine distributor in Chicago. A limousine picked me up at my hotel and whisked me out to the warehouse district where their offices are located. The chef was an Italian woman who spoke no English and one of the hosts, wearing chef's whites, was working with her on the day's menu. All of the Terlatos, who own the company, are great cooks.

For all its information, the menu failed to mention my favorite part of the meal—mashed potatoes with olive oil—which came with the main course. This dish was new to me and I loved it.

Direct import
WINE COMPANY

Luncheon for

Joy Sterling of Iron Horse Vineyards

Friday, October 29, 1993

Fresh Baked Focaccia

1990 Iron Horse Wedding Cuvee

Costolette di Maiale al Dragoncello
Pork chops sauteed and seasoned with fresh tarragon and white wine.

1992 Iron Horse Chardonnay
1989 Iron Horse Cabernets

Tossed Salad
Seasoned with Frescobaldi extra virgin olive oil and Grand Cru Vinegar
which is aged in oak for 14 months.

Espresso Coffee

7847 North Caldwell Avenue • Niles, Illinois 60714 • 708-966-9220 • Fax 708-966-9183

Mashed Potatoes with Olive Oil

Ingredients:
5 pounds Idaho potatoes
1 cup Paterno extra virgin olive oil
¼ to ½ cup hot water
2 sprigs thyme
salt and pepper to taste

Directions:
Peel and boil potatoes.

When potatoes are cooked tender, drain and put through food mill or ricer.

Incorporate olive oil and thyme while mashing with hand held potato masher.

Add hot water, a small amount at a time, to make potatoes fluffy.

Season with salt and pepper.

> From Chef Jean JoHo of The Everest,
> Chicago, Illinois

To make it at home, Forrest preheats the oven to 350 degrees, cuts a head of garlic crosswise, and roasts it until it gets soft, which takes about thirty-five minutes.

He puts two pounds of washed russet potatoes in a large heavy pot, covers them with cold salted water, brings them to a boil, and cooks them for about twenty minutes, until they're tender. He then drains them, removes the skins, and returns them to an empty pot. He squeezes out the roasted garlic pulp and adds it to the potatoes, drops in a bouquet garni of fresh thyme, sage, rosemary, and two tablespoons of whole black peppercorns, adds about two cups of water, brings it all to a boil, then reduces the heat, and lets it simmer for ten to fifteen minutes. The next step is to remove the bouquet garni, season the potatoes with salt to taste, and let them cool for fifteen to twenty minutes.

Working in small batches, he ladles the potato mixture into a food processor and purees it until it's smooth and thick like batter. Finally, he pours heavy ribbons of the puree into a serving bowl, removes any large lumps, and drizzles on a fruity, extra virgin olive oil.

About the wines, I was interested that the Chardonnay and the Cabernets, though they are in many ways opposites, worked equally well with pork chops.

Monday, October 31—Halloween. The colors around us look slightly muted, antiqued—garnet, amber, and gold mixed together in the vineyard. The wood of the bare blueberry bushes has turned wildfire red. This means the plants are lignifying, hardening off to go dormant.

For Halloween dinner, we cut a huge turban squash in half, steamed it, facedown in a baking pan with three inches of water in a 400 degree oven for an hour, then drenched it with butter and salt, and served it with a loaf of sweet bâtard from Downtown Bakery in Healdsburg and a bottle of 1989 Vrais Amis, which we had no trouble finishing. The nutty, buttery flavor of the squash was perfectly balanced by the crispness of the sparkling.

November

Feast Days: Terry's birthday, Thanksgiving

Thursday, November 3.   Forrest and I follow the Tom Sawyer theory of entertaining by putting our friends to work picking vegetables. For dessert we turn to the old pear tree with small, sweet boscs right outside our front door and the walnuts in the barn, which were harvested in October before the squirrels got them.

Forrest organizes the troops for an outing with baskets and clippers. He points out the eight varieties of winter squash, leeks, beets, cabbage, red chard, Kale, cauliflower, and Brussels sprouts, but the most exciting event seems to be digging for potatoes. It's like a treasure hunt to turn over a spade of dirt and find Yukon golds.

Today's menu for lunch at our house was potato and leek soup, green salad with our last tomatoes, bread dipped in our 1992 vintage olive oil, fruit compote, gingersnaps, chocolate wafers, and oatmeal raisin cookies.

Forrest made chicken stock for the soup the night before using a Rocky chicken (a large roasting chicken), skinned and quartered, a pound of carrots, half a head of celery, half a bunch of parsley—all from the garden and coarsely chopped, three red onions peeled and quartered, a tablespoon of coarse ground black pepper, and a tablespoon of sea salt. He covered it all with water in a large pot and cooked it over medium heat for at least two hours. "The longer, the richer," he says.

After about an hour, Forrest pulls off the whole breast, before it gets overcooked, and returns the back, wings, and legs to the broth. We'll eat the breast another day in another guise.

When the broth has cooked down to his taste, he strains it, pouring it through a colander, adds about one and a half pounds of baby potatoes and six whole leeks, coarsely chopped. How many potatoes depends on how thick you want the soup to be. Forrest uses white wine as a thinning agent. For this soup he used sparkling because that's what we had open, but we served Chardonnay at table.

Sunday, November 6. It rained for thirty-six hours straight this weekend. Six inches. A good, steady rain against a silvery sky, putting water in the creek. The ducks are happy. You can see them swishing their tails in the newly formed puddles, which soon will become natural lakes in the vegetable garden. It's surprising how quickly the leaves turn a reddish brown after a couple of frosts and some rain. You can easily pick out the warmer areas because the leaves are still colorful there.

The vineyard looks wet and muddy, a rich brown, almost black in the places where Forrest had laid out a lot of pomace, the spent skins and seeds from the press, which we use for compost. In each downpour, that beautiful topsoil runs down the culverts like chocolate milk.

Forrest is not pleased. He hasn't finished seeding the cover crop between the vines. Not that there's anything he can do about it now, except throw down sandbags to try to restrain the erosion, and wait.

Forrest has become obsessed with cover crop this year. It has been his main preoccupation since harvest ended—which kind of clover goes where, why fava beans should go here as opposed to there. The fava beans, for example, feed nitrogen back into the soil, but to get the benefit, you have to plow them under before they bear any fruit. We spend so much time talking about the soil that it suddenly hit home: "It's the soil, stupid!" so finally we're learning how to nurture it. Forrest had laid out three different kinds of lime on certain sections of the vineyard this month, but now more than likely they have been washed away, hopefully into some other part of the vineyard and not just down the creek.

A day before the rain, José had managed to change the raised flowerbeds at the entrance and all the half barrels around the winery from petunias to pansies. This for me is a sure sign of impending winter.

My choice of wines changes with the weather. Part of it has to do with the heartier fare of the season — stews call out for rich red wines — but beyond that, different facets of the wines themselves seem to emerge. Chardonnay puts us in touch with fall because it smells like apples and pears. Pinot Noir embodies the musky, earthy, nostalgic essences of fall. There's a spiciness in the air that really goes with Pinot Noir. I believe it was Keats's favorite wine.

The only incongruity in our November is the massive bouquet of red roses from the corral. If it weren't for the bowl of quince next to them, you'd swear they could occur only at the height of summer. The quince add their green-gold color to the room and a beautiful smell like spiced apples simmering on the stove.

Quince are usually for pies, jams or chutneys. Quince have a core, much like an apple, except harder and much larger. The skin is very thick so there is little meat on these fruits. Forrest has a recipe for Moroccan tagine with lamb and quince, which we love with Pinot Noir.

Forrest's Tagine

Serves 6

Ingredients:
3 large sweet onions, coarsely diced
1 bunch scallions, coarsely chopped
2 tablespoons extra virgin olive oil

3 pounds cubed lamb from a butterflied leg, as lean as
   possible, cut into 1-inch cubes
¼ cup grated fresh ginger
½ bottle red wine
2 cups water
¼ teaspoon ground black pepper
¼ teaspoon cayenne
¼ teaspoon paprika
saffron to taste
1 bunch fresh cilantro, chopped
5 quince (about 2 pounds), peeled and chopped
2 cups sliced mushrooms (white button or chanterelles)
¼ cup honey

Directions:

Sauté onions and scallions in olive oil in a big, heavy-bottomed pot until translucent. Add lamb and ginger and sauté for about 15 minutes on medium-high heat.

Add the wine and water. This time, Forrest used Pinot Noir because that's what we had left over, but any red wine would be fine.

Season with the different peppers, a pinch of saffron, and cilantro.

Bring the pot to a boil, then reduce to a simmer and cook about 30 minutes.

Add the quince and mushrooms. Let simmer another 10 minutes until the quince is soft but not mushy. Add the honey and serve with couscous, prepared according to the directions on the box.

Saturday, November 18. My parents and I flew to Atlanta for a dinner for the Chaîne des Rôtisseurs, originally a medieval guild, reborn in 1950 as an international eating and drinking society for gastronomes and food professionals, and usually devoted to French wines. This event was a Sonoma harvest dinner and we were the guests of honor. The night before, we were entertained by the head of the local chapter and her husband in their home.

It was a perfect dinner party in every way. The host and hostess had sent a car and driver to fetch us. The guest list was a lovely mix of past acquaintances and new people to meet. The menu had been carefully selected to highlight the South's finest products, and the meal was prepared by two of Atlanta's top chefs, Paul Albrecht and Kevin Rathbone, in the Halperns' home.

The serving of dinner, the silver, and the linen were just what they should have been. The wines were exquisite, French, and dizzyingly expensive. Fieuzal is the premier new-style white Graves. It's much richer and fruitier than the old-fashioned style but still keeps its minerally, steely quality. It's good with stone crab, which needs acid, and it has enough zing to stand up to Joe's mustard sauce.

Clos des Mouches is one of our family's favorite white Burgundies and with this fish course is an example of rich complementing rich.

Haut-Brion and squab are a classic combination. The texture of squab goes beautifully with the silky but firm

Howard Halpern

∞

Reception

Iron Horse Brut L.D.
Estate Bottled

∞

Dinner

Florida Stone Crabs
Joe's Mustard Sauce
1992 Chateau De Fieuzal
Pessac-Leognan

∞

Georgia Coast Baked Grouper
with Savannah Lump Crab Meat
North Georgia Mt. Stone Ground Grits
Champagne Sauce
1987 Beaune Clos des Mouches

∞

Ashville, N.C. Goat Cheese Parfait with
Atlanta's Ashland Farms Field Greens
Roasted Pecan Dressing

∞

Sumter, S.C. Squab Breast with a
medley of Black Eyed Peas,
Corn and Sweet Peas
Sweet Potato Turnip au Gratin
1982 Chateau La Mission Haut Brion

∞

Chocolate Bread Peach Pudding Souffle
with Peanut Sauce
1986 Chateau d'Yquem

texture of Haut-Brion, and 1982 is considered one of the vintages of the century for Bordeaux.

The finale was another match of very rich and rich. Every detail about this party was perfect. The crowning gesture came after coffee when the host and hostess graciously gave each guest a party favor—a fancy box of Georgia pecans, beautifully wrapped in gold paper and tied with a pretty white bow.

"There was only one thing we would have done differently," my mother commented afterward. She didn't even have to say what, because I knew she was referring to the seating. The Halperns follow American protocol, which puts wives and husbands together, something my parents forbid. They feel that if a couple wants to sit together they should stay home or book a table for two at a restaurant. The only exception might be newlyweds.

My parents like to mix everybody up. Unless formal or diplomatic protocol is called for, they prefer to seat guests according to common interests, or someone who likes to talk with a good listener, an intellectual with a very handsome man, or a judge with a journalist.

The old-fashioned rule of table talk is to alternate speaking with the people on either side of you with each course. To create even more interest, my parents frequently ask the male guests to move two places to the right after the second course, taking with them their wineglass and napkin. They feel this works best at a table for twelve or twenty-four when dinner is at least four courses. They can spend hours planning the seating using two sets of scrap place cards, setting the first round and then moving on to the second without having partners end up next to each other. If there is a protocol to observe, the guest of honor is always to the host's right, but so that every guest feels honored, Mommy always makes a point of telling whoever is on her left that he or she is closest to her heart.

My mother is deadly opposed to open seating because she feels it can turn a happy gathering hostile as soon as the first chair is tipped forward, pieces of clothing are draped over the chairbacks or somebody is spread-eagle trying to save as many seats as possible, growling if anyone unknown comes near. She prefers the luck of the draw. At large parties at Iron Horse my parents use numbered wine corks—even numbers in one basket, which are passed out to the women, odd numbers to the men, and a complete second set on the tables in sequence so everyone can just fall in.

Mother says she became sensitive to the significance of checking the seating at a party on her wedding day. The ceremony was held in the Venetian Room of the Fairmont Hotel on Nobb Hill in San Francisco. For religious reasons the wedding was timed for after sundown and for scheduling reasons it had to be done before Lena Horne appeared for the dinner show in the same room. My parents' reception was in the Gold Room—shrimp cocktail, well-done roast beef, and Orange surprise (a dessert of orange ice cream placed into a hollowed orange topped with spun sugar). The wedding cake was served with champagne in coupes—wide, low, and almost saucer shaped glasses. Mom had worked for hours on the seating but neglected to check the number of place cards against the number of invitees. Unfortunately, she forgot Aunt Rebecca, an elderly matron superstitious enough to believe that without a designated chair she was willed to die, and die she did—about twenty years later.

Thursday, November 24. Thanksgiving. Mommy called at 7:03 A.M. to tell us that Joseph Patrick, Laurence and Terry's new baby, was born at 6:58. They were ready to drive to the hospital when Mother suddenly asked if Laurence had a bottle of sparkling. "Oh, no! I forgot," he said, leaving the motor running and Terry in the front seat having contractions, all so the family tradition would remain intact—Joseph's first taste in life would be Iron Horse.

Thanksgiving is my mother's favorite holiday. Mine too. Now we have a new baby to be thankful for.

One of our Thanksgiving traditions is barrel tasting. Late morning, with the winery to ourselves, I love to wander from barrel to barrel with Forrest tasting young wines that have barely finished fermenting. This year, Laurence and his girls, Justine and Barrie, tasted with us. One was a barrel of *vin saigné*—light, fruity juice that had been "bled off" a barrel of red wine to make the red more intense. Forrest pulled out the bung, dropped a hose into the barrel, and thieved a few glassfuls. "Now, this is my idea of a turkey wine," Laurence said.

We also tried a barrel of 1994 Cabernet Sauvignon that smelled intensely like crushed violets. This is wine we spit out, carefully returning whatever's left in our glasses to the barrel because it's so delicious we don't want to lose any. Justine closed her eyes and, taking a sip, said, "It reminds me of plums." One of the advantages of tasting wines at this stage is that the fruit is at its most intense; we can more easily detect those characteristics in the wine, unobstructed by age, and they'll always be in our palate memory. This is a wine we will be drinking with friends in 1998 after two years in barrel and a year in bottle.

We sat down to table at three o'clock, which is when I imagine the original owners of this house must have dined—before it got dark. Two places were missing, Terry and Joseph. Now we'll be at least nine at table when we gather for a family meal, which my mother has concluded means that there's no use buying service for less than twelve ever again.

Joseph is actually the second addition to the family this year. The first was my mother's new knee in July, which she now says is her most valuable asset. It's a titanium implant and sets off the airport security alarms when she travels. The recuperative period was much more difficult and painful than anticipated. Father lost twenty pounds running up and down stairs for her. He did all of the exercises with her. The whole world stopped while he took care of her. She has finally regained her mobility, the pain has disappeared from her face, and this evening she and Forrest danced around the dining room table for the first time since the operation.

As soon as we got up from the table, at about six o'clock, Laurence took turkey, stuffing, and a bottle of Pinot Noir to Terry in the hospital.

We opt for Pinot Noir or Brut Rosé with turkey, but there are many possibilities. Dan Berger of the *Los Angeles Times* recommends Beaujolais Nouveau. And, citing her family's tradition, M.F.K. Fisher wrote that her mother insisted on sherry for Thanksgiving, when her father would have preferred Riesling.

It's as Narsai David said on the radio the other day, any wine is fine because there are so many different flavors in Thanksgiving, from oyster stuffing to baked yams, brown gravy, sweet onions, Brussels sprouts, glazed carrots, and cranberry sauce. Forrest suggests a wine with bright fruit and good acidity to refresh the palate during the meal. It could be Chardonnay, or Viognier might be delicious with turkey. The emotional favorite, because of its American history, is Zinfandel.

No one knows for certain, but the current theory about the origins of Zinfandel is that it was a hybridized grape developed in New York, which came around Cape Horn to California in the 1840s. At the turn of the century, post phylloxera, it was the most widely planted grape in California and remained so until 1993, when it was surpassed by Cabernet Sauvignon.

Zinfandel goes in and out of fashion. Right now it's in a resurgence, especially "old vine" Zinfandel.

The old vineyards are recognizable by the old-fashioned way they are pruned, called "head pruning," which is without trellising—that is, no wires. You can drive the tractor both ways through the vineyard as opposed to the long rows we plant now. The vines are tied to short redwood stakes and are kept to about 3 feet in height. In winter they look like gnarled, miniature sycamores. The shoots grow out of the head in the spring.

Head pruning is very conservative, not overly demanding on the vine. That and the age of the vines make production very low. Eventually economics will dictate when they will be pulled out and replanted, depending on how high the price continues to climb for the grapes.

The commercial value of a vine is at its height between twenty-five and thirty-five years of age. After that there are tradeoffs between yield and greater maturity. An older vineyard is more costly to farm, but pulling out vines is not to be done whimsically. It takes so long to get them established—three or four years to get a small first crop and at least ten years to have a mature vine. Besides the loss of crop, young vineyards will affect the style of wine that's produced. Initially their fruit will be less intense.

At a certain point in the life of every vineyard it must be replanted. I have to confess that this came as a great shock to me. I guess I thought grape vines lived forever. I have since learned the best vineyards are in a state of constant renewal. At Lafite, 5 percent of the vineyard is pulled out and replanted every year so that the average age of the vines is maintained at what they consider peak performance. There are some older vines up close to the château, but they are there more for interest, as something to look at and talk about, rather than for the wine.

Monday, November 29.   The start of pruning signifies the start of winter. The vines are completely bare. The sky is blue-gray. It's cold, damp, and foggy, typical of our weather this time of year. The hills are green again from all the rain that we've had, a muted green because of low-lying mists, very soft on the eyes. It is such a different picture from the end of harvest when the wild grasses are completely dried out and bleached almost as white as the old sheep bones scattered around T-bar-T. Mother has added pine cones and pine needles to her table decorations to mark the transition of the seasons.

We had to laugh when one of the San Francisco news anchors, after a weather live shot, said something inane like, "Gee. I would have thought the vineyards would be lush after all the rain we've had." To which the weatherman said something equally inane like, "Oh, I don't know. I'm not a winemaker." We thought it was amazing that any San Franciscan, let alone a local television personality, would thing that the vineyards would be green when they're dormant.

This is a quiet time in wine country. There are few visitors, which has its advantages for those who do venture our way because you can get a winery's undivided attention. Should you visit this time of year, I recommend packing a heavy coat and gloves, and a Stetson or something with a wide brim to keep off the rain.

It gets dark very early. Dinner at our house will be cioppino, mixed field green salad, pear and polenta tart for dessert, and a bottle of Sangiovese. The only sound outside is the clear, persistent tenors of the frogs, croaking relentlessly until dawn.

Cioppino is an old San Francisco dish. It's the very soul of North Beach Italian cooking. The main ingredients are Dungeness crab, whitefish, and bay shrimp in a tomato-based soup.

Forrest always goes overboard when food shopping. For six people, he bought three crab bodies plus about two pounds of crabmeat, a pint of crab butter (the sine qua non of cioppino though you must be very careful of freshness), one pound of shrimp, one pound of ling cod, and a pound and a half of clams. But you shouldn't feel limited. The key is fresh fish. Rock crab can be substituted. If you can't find ling cod, use true cod, or mussels instead of clams.

First, Forrest sautés one bunch of scallions, three yellow onions, and three cloves of garlic—all finely diced—in two tablespoons of olive oil. He transfers this into a big pot, adds four bags of frozen tomatoes (or four 28-ounce cans of peeled whole tomatoes), two tablespoons of chopped parsley, two tablespoons of chopped garlic chives, one teaspoon of chopped lemon thyme, two cups of white wine, and a splash of Tabasco to taste. This time, Forrest used a cup of sparkling and a cup of Chardonnay because that's what we happened to have on hand. If a recipe says to use two cups of white wine, you can choose Chardonnay, Sauvignon Blanc, or sparkling. The difference will be very subtle. Sparkling, because of it's lively acidity, will add a slightly lemony flavor.

Forrest lets the soup cook down on medium high at a slow boil until it is nicely integrated, reducing it from ten to about six cups.

After about an hour and a half, he stirs in the crab butter, adds the ling cod, and lets the soup simmer. He adds the crab, clams, and shrimp about thirty minutes before serving.

In my opinion, the perfect wine for this dish is Sangiovese.

Italian grapes have as long a history in America as anything else and in fact played a more formative role in the history of wine of this country than French grapes, despite what everyone assumes. Thomas Jefferson had a stake in an Italian vineyard in Virginia. He was an investor with George Washington and all the great families of Williamsburg — 2 acres near Monticello were planted entirely with Tuscan varietals by an Italian, Philip Mazzei, who brought ten viticulturalists from Tuscany to the Colonies in November 1773. Mazzei sold 400 shares of stock at 50 pounds each to the local gentry to provide them with their own wine.

The problem was and is today that Virginia is a very difficult place to grow vinifera grapes. Thomas Jefferson admitted defeat in 1805 and turned his attention to

native American varieties like Scuppernong and Ca-
tawba. Mazzei's Tuscan vineyard in Virginia had been
one of those eighteenth-century egalitarian experiments
that didn't work. The estate was rented to a German
general during the Revolution whose horses trampled
the vineyards.

Wine went into a deep lull after the Revolution. The
enthusiasm of translating the Old World to the New
World had waned. Then, as soon as Americans had
some money to spend, the first wines bought were
French. We looked to Europe for our sophistication. It
was the same with all of our products, including cotton.
Forrest says it took us until 1974—a great vintage,
widely considered the beginning of the golden age for
California wines—to get over the inferiority complex
we felt next to Europe.

A small wave of Italian winemakers came to Sonoma
County at the turn of the century. Some of them, like
the Foppianos, the Seghesios, and Pedroncellis, still
have their name on the door, though only a handful
were able to survive Prohibition. The Rossis, Martinis,
Gallos, and Cribaris came, according to Thomas Pinney
in *A History of Wine in America,* on the morning of repeal.

Sangiovese is a very prolific grape that can be difficult to grow because the vine wants to make more wine
than it ought to. It could comfortably produce 10 tons
to the acre and it is very labor intensive to keep the
yield lower. It requires as much due diligence as growing Pinot Noir. For example, in April, we see many
double buds—two shoots originating from the same

bud, and these must be pulled off by hand. They are very small. You can just snap them off with your fingers, but it's a lot of work. Reducing the crop intensifies flavor.

Sangiovese is a dense wine with juicy acidity. The flavor characteristics are akin to Zinfandel. Both are delicious with Italian food. Zinfandel is a little bit fruitier. The fruit that comes to mind with Zinfandel is ripe blackberries. Sangiovese is sweet-tart, like cranberries.

Zinfandel ripens unevenly, and Forrest feels the secret to making great Zinfandel is being able to judge the vineyard to bring in the right mix of overly ripe, almost raisiny fruit, perfectly mature grapes along with some percentage of underripe green grapes, so that the combined tastes have all the variations of eating wild blackberries off the vine.

The way Joel Peterson of Ravenswood, who specializes in Zinfandel, puts it is that Zinfandel should have lots of peaks. It shouldn't be round and heavy but multifaceted in your mouth.

Some of my favorite dishes with Zinfandel, besides Italian food, are grilled lamb chops and roast pork with sage, and as a component of coq au vin. The first time I tasted coq au vin it was made with a red Burgundy at Le Coq Hardy, a very famous restaurant outside Paris. For years it never occurred to me that it would be made with any other wine, but in Alsace, coq au vin is made with Riesling, so it seems only natural that in California, our version would be Coq au Zin.

Forrest pulled two single-vineyard Ridge Zinfandels

from Father's cellar—1980 Ridge Shenandoah, Amador County, and 1979 Dusi Vineyard, San Luis Obispo. It's interesting that on both labels, the appellation is simply California. They both say 13.9 percent alcohol, but have the body of wines with a higher alcohol content. Federal labeling laws allow a half a point leeway, but the limit on table wine is 14 percent. Any wine over that is in a more expensive tax class.

Ridge was founded by a group of Stanford professors and home winemakers who sought out unusual vineyards around the state to buy fruit. They were in the forefront of understanding the concept of vineyard-designated wines, Dusi being one of the greats for a particular style of Zinfandel—bold, heady, and abundantly fruity, like naturally sweet red raspberries, almost jammy. The vineyard is in the hills east of San Luis Obispo. This wine originally sold for 6 dollars a bottle.

The Shenandoah comes from Amador County, in the Sierra foothills, gold country, which was rich in Zinfandel, as was the area outside of Los Angeles near Riverside, namely Cucamonga, where the first bonded California winery was located. This wine today tastes very spicy and leathery. The label indicates that it contains 5 percent Petite Sirah. (Many old Zinfandel vineyards are really field blends with old-fashioned varieties like Carignan, Petite Sirah, and Alacante Bouche, which is the only grape that has a black skin and a black pulp.) Upon release, this bottle cost $7.50.

Forrest decanted the bottles, as there was a fair

amount of sediment. We tried the Shenandoah first and the Dusi second, while Forrest was cooking.

Glancing at Julia Child's recipe for classic coq au vin and Margaret Smith's Zinfandel cookbook, he sautéd half a pound of chopped Virginia ham and a diced sweet red onion in a large pot until the onions were translucent. He added a large coarsely chopped portobello mushroom and four smaller porcini, cubed without their stems, two cups of pearl onions, blanched whole and peeled, cracked black pepper, a pinch of dried thyme, oregano, and a bay leaf. He sautéd all this over medium heat for five minutes, then added a cup of homemade chicken broth, two cups of Zinfandel, then added a cut-up chicken, covered the pot, and let it simmer for forty minutes to an hour. This gave us another chance to assess the wines. When the chicken was done, he removed it so it wouldn't overcook, and turned the heat to high under the sauce with the ham and the vegetables. He drew out a cup of the sauce, thickened it with two tablespoons of flour, blended it until smooth, and stirred it into the pot with a tablespoon of tomato paste and salt to taste. He put the chicken back in the sauce right before serving and garnished it with chopped parsley.

At table, we poured one glass of each wine and shared them. We went back and forth on which one we preferred as the wines evolved in our glasses.

December

*Feast Days: Anniversary of the
Repeal of Prohibition,
Laurence and Terry's Anniversary,
Christmas, New Year's Eve*

On the verandas around the house, Thanksgiving pumpkins are replaced with pots of ivies, verbena, pansies, light pink and red Australian teaberries, mauve and white heathers. Citrus fruit is a traditional Italian Christmas decoration and Dad has put out dwarf Meyer lemon, Rangpur lime, kumquat, and orange trees which he plans to keep small and in containers for Christmases future. Inside the house are poinsettias, small pepper trees, branches of berries from madrona and manzanita trees, Christmas cactus with either coral pink or pale pink flowers, ginger, amaryllis, and orchids, which are timed to bloom when there's very little competition from the garden.

We feast on winter greens—chicories, kale, and cabbages, hothouse-grown mesclun and arugula. Mark relies heavily on leeks, Brussels sprouts, and fennel.

There are the last of the pears and apples to enjoy. Some of the pears are so sweet that they can be used in compotes without adding sugar, simply marinated in wine.

The pineapple guavas grown into a hedge at the rim of the orchard are ripe. We pick the largest ones and put them in a bowl on the kitchen windowsill for a few days, then cut them in half and use a demitasse spoon to scoop out the centers for breakfast.

We also have kiwi. The first vines were planted on the sound side of the Big House, twisting around the banisters of the veranda. Production is always small — two or three kiwis out of twelve vines, but they provide shade and a rather exotic effect in summer. Our best crop comes from new vines planted in full sun at the bottom of the orchard near the guavas, which yielded at least a dozen delicious kiwi in December this year.

December 3. Today marks the anniversary of the repeal of Prohibition in 1933. It's sobering to think how recent that was, how long Prohibition lasted, and how easily it could return. Hers's a toast to sanity.

By all accounts, Prohibition was the most violated law ever enacted. No one in my family paid attention to it, and a bootlegger wasn't necessarily a thug. The term was coined for men in the 1830s who hid whiskey bottles in the folds of their boots. The difference was that the bootleggers of the 1830s sold by the drink or at most by the bottle; in the 1920s and '30s they sold by the carload. Bootlegging still occurs. Many wineries sell directly to individuals, which is illegal in most states. We were bootlegging, occasionally shipping wine to friends in Texas or New York, but now the states are cracking down. They take a dim view of losing the revenue and could penalize us by revoking our license to sell at all.

FDR got the repeal pushed through by granting the states the authority to enact their own liquor laws. That was the deal. Returning that power to them was how he solidified the majority needed to enact a constitutional amendment. Ironically, Mormon-dominated Utah was the one to put the repeal over the top.

As soon as it was enacted, all the old-timers reminisce that the whole country seemed to pour into bars for their first legal drink in fourteen years. Lou Foppiano Sr., whose family winery was one of the few to survive by selling sacramental wine, remembers ordering a bourbon and water. My favorite photograph of the time is a newspaper shot of the two top federal agents in charge of enforcing Prohibition celebrating its end with champagne. Clearly, they weren't opposed to drink.

The immediate effect of the repeal was that it raised prices. A. J. Liebling complained that legal vendors were less lenient about extending credit than the bootleggers had been. Liquor and beer boomed instantly, but California wine took a long time to recover because the vineyards had been torn out.

Friday, December 9. Classic Bordeaux dinner. The morning looked very Christmasy. The ground, our deck, all the roofs were covered with frost. The live oaks are festooned with Spanish moss and bunches of mistletoe, and the persimmons, having dropped all their leaves after that first frost around Thanksgiving, now carry hundreds of cinnabar orbs that look like fat, juicy gumdrops hanging off the bare branches, the most natural Christmas tree ornaments imaginable.

Mommy dressed the table for winter. This was her second attempt. The first was lovely to look at from a standing position but was all wrong when seated at table because you couldn't see the person sitting across from you.

Now there were sprays of rosemary anchored in beautiful, very Japanese-looking tree knots, hollowed out for flower arrangements, and scattered around the table were small bunches of Lalique frosted purple grapes. The smell was beautiful and significant, as rosemary is the herb of remembrance.

I had asked for an all-Bordeaux dinner (strictly for the purposes of research for this book), and here is what we enjoyed.

Oysters with Veal Sausage on Crostini
1982 Haut-Brion Blanc

Venison Carpaccio, shaved Parmesan,
and a drizzle of olive oil
1966 Haut-Brion

Roast Pheasant with Braised Radicchio,
Steamed Potatoes, and Garlic
1964 Haut-Brion

1961 Haut-Brion

Poached Pears with Crème Anglaise
and Lace Cookies
1976 Château d'Yquem

We drank the '61 as a course unto itself. This is considered the Bordeaux vintage of the century. My father has two cases remaining out of an original twenty he had purchased as a future before we moved to France. Some of the cases were cellared in Los Angeles until we moved back to California. They have the original "Mr. Henri Selections" import sticker. The '64 and '66 were bought in France directly from the château and bear my father's import label.

Much of drinking old wines is memory. Father recalled how the '61s were delicious even when they were young. He started drinking them in the late '60s. As a result, glancing at his cellar book, you can see their rather steady consumption over the years.

We also drank in the story of Haut-Brion. It is the only classified first growth in Graves, named for its underlying gravelly soil, and the only American-owned château of the five premier grand crus, purchased by Clarence Dillon shortly after the repeal of Prohibition. The châteaus in Bordeaux were impoverished in the 1930s. Many were vying for buyers, and Dillon had his choice of Haut-Brion or Cheval-Blanc. The story is that when Dillon arrived it was a very foggy day and the ride to Cheval-Blanc too difficult, so instead Mr. Dillon went to Haut-Brion and bought that. His heiress, Joan Dillon, now a French duchess by marriage, manages the property. Before this she was a princess of Luxembourg.

Bordeaux has a strict hierarchy, fixed by the 1855 classification, which was modified only once, in 1973, to elevate Mouton-Rothschild to a first growth after twenty years of relentless lobbying by Baron Philippe de Rothschild. Cyril Ray compared the classification to the British peerage and even he, a devout claret drinker, admitted that just as in any noble family, "some generations are better than others." According to Frank Prial of *The New York Times* the château owners themselves privately discuss a reclassification. The assumption is that a number of producers would be upgraded and others stricken from the ranks, for although the vineyards endure, the châteaus change hands and the quality of their wines rises and falls depending on the work, wealth, love, passion, dedication—whatever you want to call it—invested in them. Château Margaux went through a decade-long slump until Mr. Mentzelopoulos, the Greek chain-store tycoon, restored it. The fate of Haut-Brion depends on who is next in line after the duchess. In our family, too, we look to the next generation and hope it will yield a winemaker, a moneymaker, and a marketeer.

Conventional wisdom is that the difference between

California Cabernet Sauvignon and Bordeaux is the longevity of the wines. There's a tendency to think that vintage is more important in Bordeaux than it is in California. California Cabernets are often described as having more muscle and greater fruit. Bordeaux is thought to be leaner and show more abstract aromas. It is sometimes said that the châteaus have more consistent styles while California always seems to be experimenting.

We say that winemaking has changed so dramatically both in France and the United States that we have to wait to compare, say, 1990 Bordeaux against our 1991—just in terms of longevity—because the wines are of the same era. I choose these years because 1990 was a great vintage in Bordeaux and 1991 equally so in California. Only time will tell, but for many years now, California Cabernets have bested Bordeaux or been mistaken for Bordeaux in blind tastings. They are, after all, of the same grapes, though grown in different regions, and just as Saint-Émilion differs from Graves and Graves can be distinguished from Médoc, California also has its own characteristics and within the state there are defining traits among our various growing areas.

The event that woke the world to California wine was the famous—or infamous, depending upon your perspective—1976 comparative blind tasting in Paris arranged by Steven Spurrier. Nine French judges, all wine professionals, ranked Napa's 1973 Stag's Leap Wine Cellars Cabernet Sauvignon first over the 1970s from Château Mouton-Rothschild, Haut-Brion, and

Montrose and the 1971 Léoville-Les-Cases. (For good measure, they rated a Napa Chardonnay from Chateau Montelena over some of the most prestigious French white Burgundies.)

Overall, the winemaking world has enjoyed more good to great vintages in the last twenty years than any time before. Part of that has to do with technology, both in the vineyard and the winery. Our ability to preserve wine only began with Louis Pasteur. Before that, new wine was more precious than old, because old wine turned to vinegar. This is one of the reasons why longevity has been historically a criterion of greatness. Only the greats in great years were able to last, which was especially important when you consider how long it took for wines to get to market.

Philippine de Rothschild, who succeeded her father in running Mouton, often says that it is "ridiculous" to drink a great Bordeaux any younger than 1986 today, but in reality most of our customers, and hers, are slugging down 1990s. Now, the fact that very few people have anywhere to store wine and that so much of the old vintages have been consumed has led modern winemakers to produce wines that can be enjoyed young.

Technology allows this because our presses can be employed to achieve suppleness in a young wine, whereas stomping grapes with feet extracted many more tannins—the harsh, bitter qualities—which need time to soften. If you treat a wine gently, it will be gentle.

Vintage is still very important to a winemaker. Forrest thinks of each year as new, with its own personality and pleasures. There are vintages for aging, vintages for drinking young, vintages for simple enjoyment, vintages for exploring with a connoisseur, but if you have five successful vintages in a row—within all the parameters of successful—then it's very hard to convince a traditional-minded consumer of the distinctiveness of each one.

A great vintage—when the grapes have the depth of flavor, tannin, and acid, all in perfect balance—is a quirk of fate, an act of God. As Forrest says, there's no way you can screw up. The wine makes itself. The winemaker plays a role, but is it secondary.

A truly bad vintage is a natural disaster, be it a spring frost, rain at harvest, rot, vine disease, or an infestation like phylloxera, whose latest toll in California we're only now beginning to recover from. You know a disaster as soon as it hits.

Almost as dire is a vast sea of innocuous wine that may be difficult to sell. This has become the more likely scenario as modern methods of fighting mildew, pests, and vineyard diseases have saved what in the past would have been a dead loss.

Some years can fool you. Both ways. A seemingly uninteresting vintage can develop like a swan with time. And what are touted as great years may be so tannic that, though they have the makings of greatness, they are never drinkable.

The concept of vintage is most acute in Champagne, where, because of the weather, not every year is deemed worthy of being declared a vintage year. At one house, they haven't put a year on their wines since 1990. Not declaring a vintage means a significant economic loss every year until the next vintage wine comes along. In the meantime, everything that is produced goes into nonvintage. For example, 1994 is considered "haute moyenne," high average—not exceptional, not good enough to be declared a vintage but fine for back blending with past years. Another rationalization, besides quality, is that vintage Champagne must be aged a minimum of three years on the yeast by law, nonvintage only a year and a day, and too many declared vintages would aggravate an already sizable amount of inventory stacking up in the caves.

In other regions, certain winemakers are known for being able to produce superior wines in an off year. Hubert de Montille is one in Burgundy. Christian Moueix of Pétrus and Paul Pontallier of Margaux are classic examples in Bordeaux.

It is also safe to say that every year is a vintage year somewhere in the world, when you think of the many countries producing wine today. In California, it was a major psychological hurdle for us to accept the fact that we have better weather than France. It rarely rains during harvest. California is defined by its aridity, whereas Bordeaux is quite humid in August and September, which makes it just that much more difficult to grow sound fruit. We have the luxury of thinking not just in terms of a good vintage or a poor one, but all the gradations in between.

This is all to the consumer's advantage and makes

the history of wine surprisingly democratic. We tend to think of wine as an elitist luxury, but never has so much good wine been available to so many. Actually, our "problem" in the wine world is an embarrassment of riches. People complain that there are too many wines, they can't keep track of them all, and that they feel overwhelmed by a restaurant wine list of 200 selections or a wall full of Chardonnays in a wine shop. But to say there are too many wines is like saying there are too many books. I think the analogy of wine and books is very close. And you should ask for recommendations the same way you would if you were looking for a mystery or any other genre.

Friday, December 16. Our last harvest of the year is olives for olive oil. This would be our "Michaelmas," the medieval holiday when all the crops were finally in. The morning started very beautifully. There was a shaft of light shining on the winery while the rest of the sky was light gray. The fog seemed to be lifting. We could feel that the sun was going to come out for the first time in a week.

Before building the winery, we knew we wanted our own olive trees, feeling some sort of nostalgia for the years we spent in the south of France. My parents had always gone to the old olive mill in Opio, a village in the hills above Cannes, to watch the local landowners bring in their personal crops to be custom pressed. They developed a liking for a particular style of olive oil that the French call *"fruité,"* from olives picked slightly green with higher acidity.

One of the first projects at Iron Horse was deciding where the olive trees would be planted. Instead of a grove, Father chose the long drive leading to the winery site, at that time just an old redwood barn. The trees were planted in double rows alternating with palm trees, therefore dubbed by my brother Palmolive drive. The palms were 3 feet tall and the olives did not produce for a full ten years. Today the palms stand 30 feet and our olives yield about 60 gallons of oil—about 300 bottles.

Years ago there were many olive groves in northern California. You could see them on the old estates in Napa and Sonoma. Most were torn out because olive oil was replaced by vegetable oils as a business. Hard as it is to believe now, people thought that olive oil was overly rich and unhealthy.

The bulk of the older groves that survived are Mission olives, originally introduced at the Spanish missions. Our trees, planted eighteen years ago, are mostly Mission olives. The new movement of studying olive production and experimenting with other varieties is very recent. In Europe, when we try asking Italian or French growers what type of olive trees they have, they just look at us blankly and shrug their shoulders. The trees were planted by their great-great-grandfathers.

Olive trees are alternate-bearing—abundant one year and yielding practically nothing the next. It takes ten years to get a first crop. They are harvested on the basis of color, not taste. The best-quality oil comes from olives matured to the red-ripe stage—before they turn black. Immature olives that are green or straw-colored are also gathered because they impart a unique flavor to the oil.

One of the controversies of olive oil production is how to harvest the olives. Hitting the branches with batons to knock down the fruit is supposed to be very bad because it damages the branches. Shaking the trees and letting the olives fall onto tarps laid down on the ground around the trees is said to be fine. We harvest by standing on ladders, hand-picking the olives and loading them into the same lugs we used for our grapes.

Every year there's a tug-of-war between Forrest and my parents as to when our olives should be picked. "We never argue about the wine," says Mother, "just the olives." This vintage was no exception, particularly because it was such a late year, just as it was for the grapes, but everyone in the family is very pleased with the results. It has that special, bright, south-of-France green color and peppery bite in the finish that my parents look for.

Forrest plans to bottle the 1994 olive oil in dark Italian wine bottles. Terry is designing a label and we'll use a thin black Iron Horse foil, like we use on our Cabernets, to dress it up. Forrest thinks we should hand-number the bottles—1 of 300, 2 of 300. We once signed 500 wine labels, so this will be nothing.

Saturday, December 17. Late morning we went for a hike at T-bar-T with friends. It was about as muddy a day as we could possibly have chosen.

It takes about an hour to walk the normal loop around T-bar-T. We park at the barn, going by the old family compound of a nineteenth-century farmhouse, a pool, a 1950's bungalow, and a falling-down barn that used to be a lambing shed. There are four persimmon trees that sit on the slope in front of the farmhouse. They are in their glory right now. A couple of them are very old and huge.

There's a big fenced-in vineyard that used to be horse pasture. Above it is a 20-acre-foot reservoir built in the early '50s, which you can only see when you're a quarter mile up the hill.

The view keeps broadening the higher up you climb until it includes all of Alexander Valley, the Russian River, and the hills that frame the coast. The oaks are dripping with Spanish moss and the trunks are covered with a thick emerald velvet coat like the setting for a fairy tale.

About halfway, it started to rain while the sun was shining, which my brother always says is a proof of God. We saw a rainbow forming in the mist, before it achieved any color.

I had hoped to see wild turkeys. There is a flock of about 400 at T-bar-T, not that I've ever seen one. Why, I don't know. They are large and lumbering, according to Forrest, surprisingly fast for their size, and have no predators. The coyotes are afraid of them and we certainly are no threat even with a shotgun despite the damage they cause in the vineyards. Last year they demolished Forrest's Sangiovese. It was amazing. They would stand under the vines and practically inhale whole clusters into their gullets like vacuum cleaners. It would be sweet revenge to think that the wild turkey we eat at Thanksgiving and Christmas bear some relation to the ones at T-bar-T, but the wild turkey we buy to eat is really just free range and a specific breed.

The booty from our walk included five giant branches of mistletoe, each as big as a hawk's nest, and two bins of persimmons. I took one branch of mistletoe, stuck it in a clear vase with three sprigs of bright red holly from Iron Horse for our dining room table, and scattered bowls of persimmons around our house for color. The rest we'll trade with Downtown Bakery in Healdsburg for persimmon pudding. We'll dry several batches in the oven—just sliced and put on a cookie sheet—to eat like candy and to add to compotes; others we'll use up in salads. Forrest makes a sliced persimmon and endive salad with a light vinaigrette that I adore with Brut Rosé. Some very ripe ones will go into the freezer and we will have them later like sherbet for dessert, but I think the best way to enjoy them is right off the tree on a day like today.

Wednesday, December 21. Winter Solstice. The longest night of the year, "the year's midnight," seems to demand something Druidic—beeswax candles, a ragout of black chanterelles heaped over fetuccine, bittersweet chocolate, and a reading of John Donne:

For I am every dead thing,
In whom love wrought new alchemy.
For his art did express
A quintessence even from nothingness,
From dull privations, and lean emptiness
He ruined me, and I am re-begot
Of absence, darkness, death; things which are not.

The wine for this occasion must undoubtably be a great, aged Corton-Charlemagne. A California alternative would be a fully mature Stony Hill Chardonnay.

Yesterday, anticipating spring, Father showed me clumps of daffodils already pushing out of the ground. The daffodils have naturalized and spread so that we now estimate there are more than 60,000 on the property.

Meanwhile, boxes of new bulbs are arriving daily. Father tried to restrain himself, but he claims he got "a very good deal" by rounding out his order to 1,000. Not having an inch left in his garden, he has offered to plant them around the trees in front of our house and on the long, sloping meadow behind Laurence and Terry's house.

Thursday, December 22. Forrest and I hosted the winery Christmas party at our house. Mark prepared a buffet of roast poussin, which had been rubbed with rosemary, garlic, and salt, served with olives and father's cornichons; tapenade made of olives, almonds, and orange zest; mozzarella and roasted "home frozen" pepper crostinis; rolled prosciutto filled with chicory, golden raisins, and pine nuts; *ʃuppli,* an Italian dish—breaded and pan-fried risotto balls, stuffed with ricotta salata (salty ricotta cheese); and a roulade of thin egg omelette with beautiful smoked salmon, cut like a California roll. We also served a buffet of sparkling wines—seven different cuvées lined up in a row. Everyone got one glass. We used an ice bucket for the "dump bucket," so people could taste them all—in any order they wished—or pick a favorite and stick with that. We had backup bottles of each on ice so there was no chance of running out. At a winery party, you should figure a bottle a person.

Saturday, December 24. I go back and forth on how I feel about Christmas. I truly dislike the commercialism and pressure of the holiday, though my mother says I shouldn't knock it. Part of my problem is we are so busy celebrating everything else all year long that Forrest and I feel tuckered out by the time Christmas rolls around. Left to our own devices, we would probably drive to San Francisco and go to the movies for two days straight. On the other hand, we don't want to be Scrooges—a predisposition that a reading of *A Christmas Carol* cures very quickly, giving us the heart to do what everybody does on the holidays, which is eat and eat and eat.

We woke up to a gorgeous day. It had rained all night, washing every stone on the ground perfectly clean. The sky was blue, fringed with beautiful, fast-moving white clouds and bordered by the redwoods on

top of the hill. The rain and breeze had so cleared the
air that every branch stood out in an almost surreal
way—a very Magritte effect. If we were dreaming of a
Sonoma Christmas, this was it. There was a thin carpet
of green in the vineyards—Forrest's famous cover crop.
The vine canes, having hardened off, were distinctly
rust-colored, accentuated by winter sunlight.

Most of the year, when you look across the vineyards, the trees are the background. Today, with the
vineyards bare, the evergreens, particularly the redwoods, become the focus. And there is something special about gazing through the intricate, sunlit branches
of a barren yet unpruned apple tree in the foreground
and suddenly noticing buds that are already forming.
The severity is modified by brilliant red pyracanthus
berries, primroses, pansies, and ornamental kale. Breaking the pattern totally are massive displays of camellias,
starting with Sasanquais.

Mother found one remaining red rose in the garden,
practically freeze-dried on the vine, which she added to
the camellias and ivies in her table decoration. Shake-
speare wrote, "At Christmas I no more desire a rose
than wish a snow in May's newfangled mirth. But like
of each thing that in season grows," but he didn't live
in Sonoma, where we have an eleven-month growing
season.

My mother's Christmas tree is an ivy topiary with
long, lavish tendrils, and scattered around the house
in cachepots are Christmas cacti that come out of the

greenhouse just this time of year, some with bright red flowers and others that are pale pink.

The picking list for dinner included fennel, Brussels sprouts, beets, and leeks from the garden, potatoes and onions from the barn, and chicories for salad to go with gorgeous cheeses sent to us by Charlie Palmer from his creamery in upstate New York. Most of the vegetable garden has returned to its natural role as a waystation on the north-to-south flyway for migrating birds, with dozens of winter ponds in the lower depressions filled by rain and overflow from the creek. We saw six mallards take flight as we walked up the hill to the Big House for our Christmas Eve meal. By February there will be water lilies growing here.

We gathered in the library for brioche with foie gras canapés and our choice of three champagnes: 1980 Krug Clos de Mesnil, 1990 Iron Horse Brut, and 1982 Laurent-Perrier Cuvée Alexandra. Our main course was roast wild turkey à la jardinière with 1983 Iron Horse Cabernets and 1970 Cheval Blanc. We each got a plate with four chocolate desserts—chocolate sorbet, cinnamon toast with chocolate butter, a white chocolate truffle, and a dark chocolate truffle.

Foie gras needs a very rich and full sparkling. Usually Father prefers Demi-Sec with foie gras. The Cheval Blanc was lovely by itself but didn't hold up to the main course. 1970 was one of the great recent vintages of Bordeaux, although the wines seem ready to drink now. We all preferred the Iron Horse for its fruit. 1983 was a cool, wet vintage. The wines were lean and tight when young but have opened up nicely. "This has the fruit you dream of finding in a Bordeaux but rarely do," said Father. "I guess my tastes are changing."

Sunday, December 25. Forrest took me hiking at T-bar-T. We went off the path into the hills, foraging for mushrooms in the steep wooded areas on the east side of the property where the fire had swept through this past summer. Almost all evidence of the fire was gone except for a few charred snags. The grass was green, there were hundreds of seedlings—oak, madrona, and firs that looked like baby Christmas trees—and wild iris starting to poke up in every glade. We spotted five kinds of mushrooms under the oaks, though none we'd dare eat. I loved the smell of the earth as Forrest pushed away the oak leaves. It was dense and alive like a natural compost pile that smelled like mushrooms even where we couldn't find any. Walking in this area, the mulch is so thick it feels springy underfoot. Continuing to climb, we saw a covey of wild pigeons and a wide area rooted up by feral pigs, probably looking for the same mushrooms that we were.

We sat in the sun at the top of that rise for about an hour. We nibbled on bread, cheese, tangerines, and pears that Forrest had in his backpack for a light snack. We were saving ourselves for Terry's traditional Christmas goose and 1984 Cabernet.

We slowly wound our way back down the hill along a creek, down the western side of the property, which to me looks like an enchanted forest that has been visited by fairies because of the gentle flow of water, granite mounds and boulders covered with green velvet moss, hundreds of ferns, pistachio-green lichen, and Spanish moss hanging from the oaks, swaying gently in the breeze like gray-green lace mantillas.

We eat goose but once a year—Terry's goose. It's a tradition she started when she and Laurence were married. She steams it for a half hour before roasting to seal in the juices and sweat off some of the fat. The best part of the meal are the Brussels sprouts with fried curlicues of goosefat. They're crunchy, like pork rind, sinfully flavorful, and horrifyingly fatty. Good, old-fashioned lard.

Saturday, December 31. New Year's. Ours was a very quiet New Year's—a few friends in front of a fire with two magnums of 1987 Late-Disgorged Brut, caviar, smoked salmon, and Dungeness crab.

Magnums are said to be the preferred size for sparkling. They age more slowly *en tirage* and they seem to become creamier, more the way I imagine dissolving pearls, though from a chemical standpoint I'm not sure why this is true, since the ratio of yeast to wine and the buildup of pressure are the same as in a regular 750 ml. bottle.

We each burned a hard-earned dollar bill to bring good fortune, wrote down on a piece of paper a list of things we didn't want to take into 1995 and threw them into the fire, and were so busy chatting that we missed midnight. It was as if the year never ended and we just carried on into 1995.

Warren Winiaraski of Stag's Leap Wine Cellars has a theory that you shouldn't look at any vintage on its own. He feels each year is so entwined with the next that you have to think of them together. Viticulturally, that means that the rainfall of one year affects the water table and therefore the vines' well-being into the next. Certainly the growth of the vines in a year sets the framework for what you have to work with in the following vintage, and psychologically, the successes and failures of one year set the pace for the next.

At Laurence and Terry's annual New Year's Day party, I was struck by how many people had resolved to slow down and enjoy life more. I was most delighted to hear from one person — a winemaker, in fact — that his New Year's resolution was to drink more sparkling wine, something I think we'll all be doing as the realization hits home of how close we are to the turn of the millennium. If the prospect of the year 2000 doesn't usher in a feeling of hope, what will?

Epilogue

It started raining on January 3. In nine days we received thirty-six inches, more than we expect in an entire year. I felt guilty that I was away from home, poolside in Miami. When I called in, my brother told me, "It's Day Five of the deluge. The good news is that there are only thirty-five more to go." I could only hope that Iron Horse was the designated ark.

Forrest lost about 250 vines—about a third of an acre—that slid off a hill at T-bar-T. The erosion caused a hole 8 feet deep. The vines were planted only last spring and since these storms were uprooting redwoods, there was no way they could hold on.

Iron Horse is simply a mess. The bridge flooded three times. We were often without power. The ranch road was washed away, the vegetable garden is a lake—that's why there's no vineyard there—and we are way behind on pruning. There's absolutely nothing we can do until the ground dries out.

We got off easy because we're all hillside vineyards, and the fava beans Forrest was so passionate about planting last fall held up our topsoil. During the worst of the storms you could stand by the end of a row and catch clean water in a glass.

Forrest will replant the steep section he lost at T-bar-T. The road will get repaved. The seeds and bulbs will wait in the barn where it's dry and dark until they can be planted.

Wednesday, January 16. I saw two red crocus at the corner of the barn and one daffodil in front of our house. Wild narcissus is popping up all around T-bar-T. That's three wishes and the start of a new growing season.

Addendum

With six adults in my family, there are at least six opinions on any given wine and food question—sometimes more. Here are some of our personal ideas of what works well together as well as some of our favorite wines other than Iron Horse.

Blanc de Blancs: oysters, smoked fish, fish carpaccio, imperial rolls with shrimp, coriander, mint and peanuts, scallops, abalone, fish chowder, white asparagus, sweet, sliced melon

Taittinger Comte de Champagne Blanc de Blancs, Salon, Scharffenberger

Blanc de Noirs: smoked salmon, tuna tartare, crab cakes, fresh-baked focaccia, herb and mushroom soup, grilled rabbit and mashed potatoes, chicken cooked with tamarind, potatoes, lime leaf and coconut milk, warm pear tart with honey ice cream

Gloria Ferrer

Brut: sushi, tempura, prosciutto, Dover sole and champagne sauce, champagne risotto, vegetable pizzas

Veuve Clicquot Yellow Label, Krug

Brut Rosé: steak, tuna, lobster, salmon, rouget fillets with stuffed zucchini flowers, Caribbean fish stew, lamb with mint and tomato, ham, turkey, grilled duck breast, veal and watercress

Billecart Salmon Rosé, Laurent-Perrier Cuvée Alexandra

Demi-Sec: foie gras, wild strawberries and vanilla sauce, apple-cinnamon buckle, fresh fruit tarts

Gewürztraminer and Riesling: green chilies and smoky foods—particularly smoked chicken, Thai, Szechuan, Indian food—anything with a little kick, foie gras with roasted figs, creamy cheese and bosc pears

Domaine Zind-Humbrecht and Trimbach Cuvée Frédéric Émile of Alsace

Sauvignon Blanc or Fumé Blanc: oysters, clear fish

soup, soft-shell crab, grilled lobster, Hawaiian cuisine, Asian dishes with tropical fruits and spicy tones, Italian antipasti, Provençale dishes with tomatoes, thymes, and basils, tapenades, pork and crab red curry sausage, (Stephen Pyles makes a salmon in hoja santa, a Mexican herb with a slight anise flavor, which is delicious with a grassy-style Sauvignon Blanc), anything with apples, like salmon with an apple and mint sauce, anything with fennel

Rochioli and Hanna from Sonoma, Cloudy Bay is the most famous Sauvignon Blanc from New Zealand. We also like Hunter and one called Forrest, which we first tried just for the name. Bordeaux is producing more whites. Blanc de Lynch-Bages is delicious but very expensive.

Chardonnay: a clean, crisp style of Chardonnay with oysters, pancetta and cream sauce over pasta, Maine lobster steamed with butter or à l'Américaine, corn and seafood chowder, grilled halibut, shrimp, prawns sautéd in butter, abalone, scallops, sea bass, pheasant, quail, pork loin with fresh peach chutney

Ferrari-Carano, Kistler, Simi Reserve, Silverado, Girard

Pinot Noir: meaty fish like tuna, swordfish, salmon, and sturgeon, salade niçoise, grilled baby chicken with mushrooms and spinach, white meats (veal and pork), herb-crusted rack of lamb, white meat game birds (quail, partridge), duck, wild mushroom pasta, beef and green chili enchiladas, smoky dishes, foie gras on toasted gingerbread

Williams Selyen, Rochioli, Etude. Both my husband and my father love the wines from a particular vineyard, Clos des Chênes, in Volnay, Burgundy.

Cabernet Sauvignon: either a young, light-style or a mature Cabernet with squab, roast pork loin with dried cherry sauce, lamb with artichokes and olives, beef, roast venison, antelope, buffalo, cheese

Caymus, Dunn, Berringer, Geyser Peak Reserve, Robert Mondavi Reserve, Clos Pegas

Zinfandel: catfish with black pepper, pan-roasted squab breast with baked sweet potatoes, grilled lamb, ratatouille

Fritz, Nalle, Rafanelli, Ravenswood, Ridge, Rosenblum

About the Author

Joy Sterling is the author of *A Cultivated Life* and serves as the director of sales, marketing, and public relations at Iron Horse Vineyards. She was raised in Paris by American parents, graduated from Yale, and had a ten-year journalism career before joining the family winery in 1985. She is married to Forrest Tancer, Iron Horse's winemaker, and they reside at the vineyard, located outside Sebastopol, California, in Sonoma County.